DATE DUE

NO 2 4 '93			
DE 1 0 '93			
NO 2 8 '94			
DE 1 6 '94			
DE 1 6 '96			
AP 7 '97			
NO 4 '98			
DE 9 '98			
AP 2 4 '00			
MR 2 1 '00			
MY 22 '02			
JE 7 '02			

DEMCO 38-296

AN INTRODUCTION TO TEAM-APPROACH PROBLEM SOLVING

AN INTRODUCTION TO TEAM-APPROACH PROBLEM SOLVING

Louis N. Jones
Ronald C. McBride

ASQC Quality Press
Milwaukee, Wisconsin

AN INTRODUCTION TO TEAM-APPROACH PROBLEM SOLVING

Louis N. Jones
Ronald C. McBride

Library of Congress Cataloging-in-Publication Data

Jones, Louis N.
    An introduction to team-approach problem solving / Louis N. Jones,
Ronald C. McBride.
        p.   cm.
    Bibliography: p.
    Includes index.
    ISBN 0-87389-061-2
    1. Problem solving, Group.   2. Quality circles.   3. Work groups.
I. McBride, Ronald C.   II. Title.
HD30.29.J66   1989
658.4'036—dc20

Acquisitions Editor: Jeanine L. Lau
Production Editor: Tammy Griffin
Cover design by Artistic License. Set in Plantin by DanTon Typographers.
Printed and bound by Edwards Brothers.

ISBN 0-87389-061-2

Printed in the United States of America

ASQC Quality Press
310 West Wisconsin Avenue, Milwaukee, Wisconsin 53203

TABLE OF CONTENTS

FOREWORD

The problem with forecasting the future is that the future is not what is used to be.
Anonymous

While I would hesitate to argue with the conventional wisdom that history repeats itself, I doubt that it was a thought born in corporate America. Unless, of course, we think of change. Little else is more certain for the future.

If quality has been a major element of conceptual change in this decade, properly forced upon us by Japanese industry, then it will be something else in the next. For to survive, the need to match a uniform global quality of product and service will be axiomatic and the hallmarks of innovative winners are likely to emerge as productivity, manufacturing flexibility, price, and marketing skill on a global basis. Who knows, today, precisely what Perestroika, Europe 1992 and Greater China will bring us in terms of global marketing opportunities and problems to be solved?

The authors of this intensely practical book have personally lived and, almost, commercially died through a period of massive change. They have documented this experience, littered with failure but never despair, to present readers with a hands-on summary of invaluable lessons learned the hard way. They hope that this book will be a living guide to others who will need to solve the problems that continue to emerge in the future.

Of particular relevance is their frequent reference to culture. Alteration of industrial behavior patterns, or culture, is primarily what problem solving in the context of this book is all about. And yet to change a corporate culture, without a wholesale change of management, is the greatest challenge of all.

As we move along the path from a quality born of *handcrafted with pride* and personal service to the productive precision of smart machines and the information age, a significant culture change is clearly implied. The authors handle this issue by never letting the reader forget that it is people who solve problems, and the process of solution must never neglect their values, fears, and emotions while using their skills, desires, and intelligence.

K. Grahame Walker

PREFACE

Failure is the back door to success.

W. Chaffin

During the early 1980s we worked in classic quality management for a specialty chemical company that supplied products to the electrical and electronic industries. One of our company's major products was sold to the semiconductor industry which was feeling the pressure of increased competition, especially from the Japanese. Our management was committed to gaining market share by improving the quality of our products, service, and people.

During our initial efforts to improve quality we established quality circles, task forces, and self-managing teams. However, we encountered several problems, including:

- Failure to obtain long-lasting, positive results

- Use of generalized techniques that did not correct the root causes of problems.

- Failure to see team involvement as enjoyable, meaningful, and productive

Eventually, through successes and failures, we identified and developed practical processes that can be useful to others as they pursue a quality improvement strategy. The team approach to problem solving is one of these processes. It includes a six-step method for team building and increasing team dynamics. This system, named DISTIL, combines creative, judgmental, and logical approaches to move a team from problem identification to a long-lasting, positive solution.

The procedures worked for us and we would like to share them with all those dedicated to working together toward improved quality.

Louis N. Jones
Ronald C. McBride

ACKNOWLEDGMENTS

We gratefully acknowledge the following who helped us in various ways with this project:

- *K. Grahame Walker*, President, Chief Operating Officer, The Dexter Corporation, who encouraged us to start Quality Technics, a quality training and consulting business within Dexter.

- *T. Daniel Clark*, President, Mogul Division, The Dexter Corporation, who championed the formation of Quality Technics and gave us constant support.

- *Our colleagues*, HYSOL Division, The Dexter Corporation, who helped us form and refine our teamwork and problem-solving skills during our many years with them.

- *Jeanine Lau*, ASQC Quality Press, who encouraged us to write this book and helped us publish it.

- *Harrison White* and the staff at BLAIR, TOWNE & BINGHAM, Olean, NY, who prepared our first edited draft.

- *Kate McBride*, our secretary, who typed the first manuscript and put up with our many changes and additions.

- *Millie Jones*, for innovative ideas, encouragement, and support.

1
PREPARING AN ORGANIZATION FOR TEAMS AND TEAMWORK

ORGANIZATIONAL CHANGES

Organizations today are stressed increasingly by the need to improve profits, productivity, and quality. Meeting these challenges requires dynamic changes in all aspects of the organization to ensure economic survival. Organization change means not only the implementation of varied programs, processes, and improvements, but also requires alteration of the corporate culture.

Toffler[1] recognized the importance of human involvement in his classic book, *Future Shock*, when he stated, "It is important to look at it (change) closely, not merely from the grand perspective of history, but also from the vantage point of the living, breathing individual who experiences it." Naisbitt's[2] *Megatrends* deals extensively with the changes required today and in the future as America shifts from an industrial-based economy to one that is service- and information-based. Other outlooks and insights into generalized change have been provided by Kanter,[3] Ouchi,[4] and Peters.[5]

To meet the stresses of today and the challenges of the future, many organizations are becoming more participative by involving employees more and more in decision making. Currently, one approach used for economic survival is the team effort. Teams are groups of individual employees who work together for a common cause.

In preparing an organization for teams, it is important to understand the corporate culture. Teams can be successfully introduced into cultures that range from autocratic to participative styles. The secret is to make the team program match the cultural pattern rather than conflict with it. Once participative management begins to grow and prosper in an organization, it will naturally alter the culture and its people.

The lack of adequate planning is a major cause of failure in the implementation of teams in an organization. Once the decision to use teams has been made, it inevitably requires drastic changes. These changes will affect not only the physical and structural aspects of the work life, but will require a cultural alteration of every sector of the work force. Even when the theory is understood and applied, at some critical point the concepts and approaches to teamwork will meet, collide, and conflict with entrenched organizational systems. Failure is often attributed to factors such as lack of middle management involvement or insufficient commitment by top management, but in reality, these are generally just symptoms of the root cause, i.e., poor preparation.

Sometimes team-driven programs are introduced into an organization with much fanfare, fueled by early enthusiasm, and justified by dollar savings from early successful projects. However, once the "honeymoon" is over, various failure modes begin to appear. Failure does not, or at least should not, mean the end of team activities, for "failure is the back door to success." Failure, when properly understood and dealt with, can energize a program.

Rather than terminate a failed team program, it's more appropriate to treat it just as we would treat a failed mechanical device, i.e., subject it to a systematic examination to identify and analyze the probability, causes, and consequences of potential and real failure. This extensive study often indicates that failure is related primarily to the following key items:

1. Drastic fluctuations of business; that is, both up and down fluctuations produce negative results.

2. Lack of active involvement and true understanding from middle management.

3. Loss of a high-level "champion."

4. Noninvolvement of staff in service areas of the division.

PREPARING AN ORGANIZATION FOR TEAMS

Rather than waiting for a person to get sick, a product to fail, or a system to break down, it is better to take steps to prevent the unwanted situation from occurring. To prepare an organization for teams, the organization must move from a failure/detection mode to a success/prevention mode. Preparing for participative management, statistical process control, total quality control, etc., are all subsets of preparing an organization for change, a process covered in more detail in *Human Resource Management.*[6]

Change is not only the implementation of many different programs and systems, but it entails a cultural alteration. People are not only physically and mentally stressed by change, but change has a strong emotional impact. Our prescription for change is offered not as a cure-all miracle drug, but as a set of basic principles which should be understood, evaluated, and applied only as required.

1. Plan Before You Plunge

W. A. Golomski, consultant and former president of the American Society for Quality Control, states that, "There are some critics who feel that long-range plans are of little value because conditions change rapidly and make them useless. . .others feel that plans should be constructed to enable you to seize opportunities."[6] Extensive planning is a key ingredient in the successful introduction of a team's program. All levels of the organization should be represented in the planning stage. The steering committee, in conjunction with a coordinator, should undergo training, be actively involved with evaluating other team programs, determine general employee attitudes via extensive surveys, and determine the type of inside/outside training resources the organization requires. To properly plan for teams, the committee must have the answers to questions such as:

- Who will be responsible for implementing the team program?

- Will teams be introduced throughout the organization simultaneously?

- What resources will be required to handle the implementation?

- How will teams and teamwork affect all areas of the operation?

2. Don't Crusade Alone

The great change agents such as Martin Luther King, Ghandi, and Jesus were destroyed as they attempted to implement change. If change is too strongly associated with a single individual or a small group, emotional opposition or indifference will negatively affect the program.

3. Bring Everyone on Board

Appropriate communication pathways must be established to properly explain the proposed change. Training may be required to ensure that various factions see and understand "what's in this for me?"

4. Be Sensitive to the Impact of Change

Plans made in the paneled conference room may affect the workers on the shop floor in unforeseen ways, unless their concerns are thoroughly examined. While the physical impact of change is often addressed directly, the mental or emotional impact frequently is forgotten or minimally considered. The knowledge gained by a thorough assessment of all predictable outcomes of change should be merged into the training and implementation plans.

5. Implement the Entire Strategy, Not Just the Slogan

Control charts posted throughout the production area and banners draped over the cafeteria walls may be outward indicators of change, but many times signs, slogans, charts, and awards are just fluff. These instruments are important aspects of statistical process control (SPC) when properly used. However, they can be a negative factor if not properly used and accepted.

6. Measure, Monitor, and Modify

To succeed with a new process or program, an organization should establish a baseline or work mark by measuring its culture before implementing a specific change. Planning must include ways of measuring attitudes as well as actions. Planning should also include accepted ways of modifying the goal.

7. Use Time as a Tool

Quality improvement and its related processes require time measured in years, not months. If short-term results are emphasized, time will become a negative factor. Employees may feel that they are being pushed, not consulted. Employees at all levels require time to become accustomed to, and familiar with, change. Properly planned goals, with options agreed upon during the planning stage, can ensure that time becomes and remains a positive factor.

8. Reinforce Desired Behavior

In their book, *Choosing Success*, Jongeward and Seyer[7] point out how desired behavior can be reinforced by nurturing employees through a process called "stroking," i.e., giving employees some kind of recognition. Good strokes humanize and improve the quality of work life. During change, workers require positive strokes in many varied forms, from a simple "thank you" to formal awards. Positive reinforcement is especially needed just before and just after that ground zero point where the change theory is turned into practice.

9. Nail Down the Implementation

Many quality programs get off to a good start with an abundance of flag waving and good intentions, but then silently disappear in a cloud of neglect and inattention. A highly visible plan for implementation should contain carefully outlined steps, target dates, objectives, etc., which are communicated to employees at all levels.

10. Integrate the Change into the System

As long as a special program stands out, it is in danger of being constantly attacked, diluted, or even eliminated. Changes should be quickly and quietly assimilated into the existing system and organizational culture. When the change becomes part of the operational norm, the prescription for change will have achieved the desired results.

TECHNIQUES FOR CHANGE

A detailed description of the planning and implementation of a total quality management system for The HYSOL Division of The Dexter Corporation is described in *Human Resource Management?* Some of the key concepts include:

Perspective — The perspective adopted is entitled, "Directed Total Participation (DTP)." In this approach, once a program has been created, tested and accepted by management, it is introduced to the total organization as a process for everyone, similar to the medical insurance or profit sharing plan. It is participative in that each person can elect to be active or inactive, but it is directed in that, as a top-down process, it dictates that everyone should be involved in the process.

Organizational Change — To provide a backbone for DTP, a new type of organizational structure is created. This system, called integral management, combines teamwork, participative management and traditional decision-making systems into a new, interlocking system of teams, including quality circles, task forces, and project teams.

Evaluation — To obtain the involvement, commitment and input of the entire organization, a quality awareness survey is conducted. Not only is the employees' input gathered before implementing the process, but top management makes a definite commitment that it demonstrates by taking action in response to employees' input.

Training — A training system is installed for all levels, from top management to factory floor. Subjects include items as diverse as teamwork, communication, creative problem solving, SPC, quality costs, human factors engineering, etc.

Incentives — After investigating Scanlon type plans, Rucker plans, and Improshare plans, a profit-sharing plan, in which monetary incentives are tied to quality improvement, is established. The profit-sharing plan is reinforced by other nonmonetary recognition incentives.

Communication — A communication matrix is created to increase effective communication across all levels of the organization. It includes such items as top management letters, division and operational newsletters, and team publications.

By taking the first letters of the six factors just discussed, the acronym POETIC is formed. Poetic work is defined as the art of creating a language of imagination expressed in verse. Good or bad poetry cannot be adequately defined as merely putting together certain metered lines, because there are many indefinable properties that distinguish good from bad poetry.

The same is true for defining a program to handle change. The proper implementation of this process requires quality techniques, but without thought, insight, creativity, and emotional involvement of individual employees, change in an organization's system and culture will be difficult or impossible to achieve.

2
BUILDING THE TEAMS

Few teams develop to their full effectiveness without a good deal of nurturing and conscious development.

Francis Ana Young

When an organization begins to implement teams and teamwork as a means of spreading participative management, there will usually be a few who ask, "Why teams?" For some people, teams, task forces, quality circles and committees mean simply the gathering together of a group of people who collectively make decisions that will accomplish little or nothing. When you look at how unproductive, dull, and boring some group meetings are, it's not surprising they are held in such low regard.

Why teams? Dr. Thomas Gordon, in his book, *Leader Effectiveness Training*, has answered the question with the following seven steps:

1. Members of an organization will be identified more with the goals of the organization and concerned about its success if they participate in making decisions about those goals and how to reach them.

2. Being a member of a management team gives group members a feeling of greater control over their lives; it frees them from the fear of the leader's arbitrary use of power.

3. When group members participate in solving the group's problems, they learn a great deal about the technical complexities of whatever the group's task is; they learn from each other, as well as from the leader. Developing a management team is the best kind of ongoing staff development (inservice training).

4. Participation on a management team provides opportunities for the members to satisfy many of their higher-level needs for self-esteem, acceptance, and self-actualization.

5. A management team helps break down status differentials between the members and the leader, which fosters more open and honest communication between members and leaders.

6. A management team becomes the principal vehicle enabling the leader to exemplify the kind of leadership he or she wants the group members to learn and use in relationships with their subordinates. In this way effective leadership moves down through the levels of organizations.

7

7. Higher-quality decisions often result from bringing into play the combined resources of the work group.

TYPES OF PARTICIPATIVE GROUPS

Teams and teamwork may take many forms, from executive teams composed of top management, through action teams composed of middle management, to quality circles and other worker participative groups for line employees. It is vital that teams be interlocking parts of the organizational systems, not special units.

MANAGEMENT TEAMS

Management teams usually produce a people-centered system in which problems are dealt with and solved by a systematic, data-based focus on decision making. Many of the problems faced by management teams are interdepartmental and deal with quality, productivity, and cost saving. Solving these types of organizational problems requires a data-based nonemotional approach. Management teams should be created to include all responsibilities associated with the problem. It is important that recognition be oriented toward the teams, not the individual managers or departments. The commitment to management teams must be from the top down. Senior managers should use multilevel teams rather than direction and command to achieve their personal wishes and goals. Management teams need training, reinforcement, and support. It takes time, commitment, and understanding to create effective, efficient management teams.

ACTION TEAMS

Action teams are usually composed of members from various departments and levels, usually brought together to achieve a specific goal within a deadline. The scope of the assignment and the time frame will, of course, vary greatly depending upon the organization and the problem. In many cases, management will have set priorities and identified the group's task before the group is formed. These groups will often be assigned to work full time on the problem until it is solved. Many are temporary in nature and when the solution is achieved, the teams will disband or become nonfunctional.

QUALITY CIRCLES AND OTHER PARTICIPATIVE GROUPS

Quality circles are groups of workers who voluntarily meet on a regular basis to identify, analyze, and solve quality (and other) problems. Ideally, members are from the same work area or do similar work so that the problem they select will be familiar to all of them.

Workers' participation in circles should be voluntary in order to avoid the feeling of being pressured to do a "management thing." While circles usually work with clear guidelines, it's important for them to choose their own problems based on their needs. As much as possible, circles need to feel they are working without time pressures on a long-term basis to achieve lasting solutions. Circles are not an appropriate way to deal with a crisis. Circles are most successful when they become a permanent part of the way the organization operates. They need assistance and guidance to ensure that they can solve problems in an efficient and acceptable manner.

TEAM BUILDING VIA TAPS

Once an organization has made the decision to implement teams, it is necessary to obtain training materials, train team leaders, and select team members. Participants are brought together, trained, and given or allowed to select appropriate problems. Faced with a problem to solve, the group of individuals looks from one to the other and realizes that they are not a team, but a group of individuals trying to work together. Meanwhile, throughout the entire organization, management at every level loudly and proudly proclaims that teams are now actively working.

This scenario has been repeated over and over again in too many American organizations. Many of the failures of circles and other participative groups can be traced to the fact that they never truly became a team. Of course, some groups do serendipitously become a team, but this is chance, and certainly not efficient.

The team approach to problem solving, TAPS, evolved out of the frustration and failures of working with quality circles, quality of work life groups, and corrective action teams. Rather than assume that a group of individuals brought together to solve problems are a team, it is better to take the "null hypothesis" that they are not a team and to provide them with help.

TAPS provides a group with three important elements: team building skills, team dynamics, and team problem-solving methodology. TAPS is not only designed to make the team efficient and effective, but more importantly, it provides a vehicle for improving the interpersonal relationships of the group. For many, its chief feature is that it is an enjoyable experience.

A team has been defined as *an energetic group of people who are committed to achieving common objectives, who work well together and enjoy doing so, and who produce high quality results.* If this is so, then team building is a process by which a group of individuals bonds together to become a unit.

Can you imagine a U.S. Marine drill instructor accepting a bunch of newly head-shaven recruits as a Marine team? Of course not, but after enduring a process designed to produce Marines, those individuals who remain in the program will be ready and willing in a matter of weeks to risk their lives for another buddy or even another unknown Marine.

We are not suggesting that night marches through swamps and infiltration drills under fire are necessary to forge individuals into a team. However, we are saying that team building requires construction and implementation of a plan to ensure a good foundation for team success.

While a team can be as small as two or as large as an entire company, we will focus on the classic team comprised of six to 10 individuals. As individuals, the new team members bring not only their skills, hopes, and innate intelligence to the experience, but they also bring their values, fears, and emotions. As individuals they want to find the answer to such questions as:

- What am I here to do?

- Who's in charge?

- How will I fit in with others and the group?

- How will the team operate?

- What's in this for me?

and other similar "I" related concerns.

If these concerns are not brought to the surface, addressed, and answered, they may become barriers to the team building process, both for the individual and the group. Those who have endured the military's team process know that questions such as those raised above are answered directly and openly, with little chance for misinterpretation. However, in many teams, groups, and circles, leaders and members are so concerned with alienating others, especially in the early stages of the team, that they politely overlook or intentionally pass over these needs.

Teams need a building process that is planned, described, and mutually understood. The TAPS team-building process provides for groups to mutually proceed through four defined stages of development — from a loose group of individuals to a dedicated team. Some groups will naturally follow a satisfactory team developmental pathway, but our approach is designed to ensure that all bases are touched. If natural circumstances do not produce the needed experience, TAPS provides the leader with structured activities and guidelines to provide the experience.

Stage one: the mirror stage. The initial stage is one of questioning and testing. Individuals are holding up a mirror in two positions. First, they position the mirror to reflect their own image as they try to find their place in the group. Then they turn the mirror to reflect the image of the other group members who see themselves rather than the person holding the mirror. Each of us has a personal way of getting involved. Some will jump right in with humor, openness, and conversation while others hold back until they feel more comfortable with the group and the group surroundings. Structured team exercises help by allowing individuals both to look at themselves and to share with others in a nonthreatening atmosphere.

Stage two: the one-way window stage. As a team develops it moves into a stage characterized by conflict and infighting. Alliances and cliques are formed as influence and power tend to direct the interpersonal relations. This is often a critical period for the team leader as well as for the team. It is, however, an opportunity for the leader to establish the norms which can provide for future successful team performance. Members will be closely observing the leader and the leader's actions while they are trying to decide whether to accept the leadership or begin to develop *invisible agendas* designed to evade or overthrow existing leadership. Outsiders observing a team actively involved in this stage may conclude that the team is in trouble or is failing. In some instances, management has terminated teams going through this stage even though it was in reality a normal part of the group building experience. Leaders, facilitators, or team-building consultants must ensure that teams successfully complete this stage so that it will not provide a fundamental weakness later in the group's operating life.

Stage three: the two-way window stage. Once the group has resolved the stage two concerns, it can use its energy and direction to tackle problem solving. By this time people have committed themselves to making the team work, they give up some of their individual properties to the group, and they really want to work together. For a military team this is when everyone is in step and moving to the same external and internal cadence. TAPS provides the team with structured ways to identify its precision and its contribution. The team develops methods of listening, being creative, and handling problems in a flexible and effective manner. This stage takes time, for a group must develop its own way of working together and interacting. Common goals and making decisions by consensus begin to be practiced as a team way of life.

Stage four: the open window stage. When a team reaches this stage of maturity many fears and doubts have been eliminated or recognized and controlled.

The team members have developed a closeness and openness which allow them to share themselves with each other and enjoy doing it. Members know their roles and a definite bond holds the group together. It is in this stage that the team can most efficiently solve problems by working together.

TEAM DYNAMICS

Understanding team dynamics — the very complex way individuals interact with one another — is an important foundation for building a successful team. When it's finally time to decide whether a team or circle program has been successful, no measure of improvement can be accurate unless it gauges team dynamics.

Elementary chemistry teaches us that atoms come together and bond only when and if there are conditions where the system energy required after bonding is less than the total individual energy required before. While this is, of course, a vast simplification of chemical reactions, it is certainly the basis of the *win-win* concept that serves to promote team dynamics. Individuals share their energies with the team because by doing so the total entity can improve.

With chemical bonding theory as a background, TAPS was created to provide individuals and the group with verbal and nonverbal ways of sharing their energies. Leaders are provided with guidelines on how to recognize when stress, irritation, worry, distraction and other out-of-order feelings are interfering with the team dynamics. TAPS also provides a proven method to allow individuals or groups to work their way out of this undesirable situation.

TAPS METHODOLOGY: DISTIL

Even when a team has matured and is dynamically prepared to solve problems, it is still necessary for that group to work with a defined method which will allow the team to properly and permanently resolve the problem. Figure 2.1 shows the ideal situation a team should encounter when trying to solve a problem.

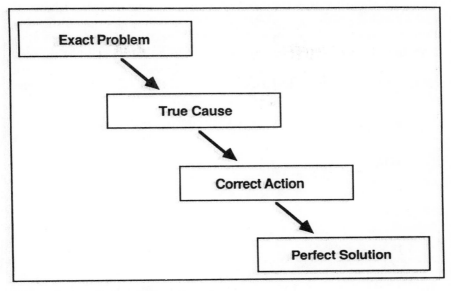

Figure 2.1   Ideal problem situation.

The ideal team situation is to be confronted by an exact problem which has a true cause. If the team can find that true cause and apply the correct action, the result will be a perfect solution. However, most problems follow the pathway indicated in Figure 2.2, where rather than encountering an exact problem, the team must deal with a *big mess*.

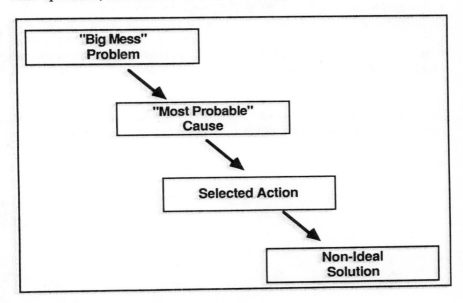

Figure 2.2   Usual problem situation.

When faced with a complex mixture of liquids in the chemical laboratory, one of the methods of separating the ideal solution is by distillation. DISTIL, which is an acronym for the TAPS method of taking a problem from the *big mess* state to final resolution, works on the most probable cause. DISTIL applies a selective alternative to achieve a non-ideal but workable solution to the problem. The six major steps of the TAPS' DISTIL process are:

- Definition

- Image

- Selection

- Test

- Implementation

- Longevity

DISTIL contains many of the elements found in popular problem-solving methodology, such as Kepner-Tregoe and quality circle problem solving. But the elements are combined in a different manner, with the addition of less familiar problem-solving devices. DISTIL blends techniques such as brainstorming, cause-and-effect analysis, and priority analysis with other creative and selective tools, such as affinity analysis, imaging and flow diagramming to create a concerted problem-solving approach. DISTIL also includes some unique elements that provide flexibility, team synergy, and group involvement in a game-like environment. This technique uses a minimum of theoretical training by workers in quality circles, engineers and scientists in study groups, multilevel corrective action teams, and management teams.

The individual steps of DISTIL are discussed and further explained in the chapters that follow. A case example is presented in the appendix.

3
DEFINING A PROBLEM

A problem well defined is half solved..."

Anonymous

GENERAL

The objective of the definition step in DISTIL is to reduce one general problem to a specific problem that, if corrected, would have a significant impact. The solution may save dollars, increase production, or improve bottom-line profits. The solution may also help employees feel better about themselves, cut down on absenteeism and complaints, or generally create a better lifestyle in the work place for everyone. Whatever the desired effect, the real point is that a problem must be properly defined before it can be solved. Too often we make the quantum jump from understanding that we have a problem to the point of suggesting a solution and implementing it. However, the real world does not usually hand us a well-defined problem. Most of us usually must deal with a messy situation, one which involves symptoms, related factors, unrelated outside factors, and possible causes. In short, we face not a single problem, but rather a *big mess*. Too often we make our first assessment of a *big mess* but then stop there, or concentrate on one of the extraneous factors.

To solve problems effectively, we must first reduce our views, or the group's views, of the problem to a specific set of factors. In order to do that, we must employ a means of defining the problem. The statement has been made that a problem properly defined is 98 percent solved. The numbers in this equation may not be correct, but certainly it is important to properly reduce the *big mess* to a specific problem before trying to solve it.

Experts in the field of problem solving generally identify three distinct types of problems — analytical, judgmental, and creative. However, these are not distinct, separable types, but they are always a part of any problem-solving process. In the balance among these types, the dominant one usually determines how we perceive the problem type. There is, however, enough difference among them and in the proper approach to them to discuss them separately.

Analytical problems are those which have a definitive answer, one which can be reached using mathematics and strict logic, such as the problem of determining how many apples are in a bushel. This problem can be solved by simply counting the apples is some predetermined way or estimating the apples by taking a sample and then predicting how many remain. This method may become extremely difficult and may require all types of sophisticated techniques, instrumentation, and statistics to determine the answer. But the fact is, in analytical problems, there is a definitive, single answer. It is simply a matter of how best to reach it.

The second type of problem is judgmental. This calls for a decision between right or wrong, moral or immoral, yes or no. This is often recognized because "should" is frequently the key word in this type: Should we paint the room red or white? Should we go to the movies tonight or stay home? Should I keep Thomas on the payroll or fire him? We are often faced in the everyday world with making judgmental decisions. We must be able to recognize judgmental problems as we go through the definition stage.

The third type of problem is creative. Creative problems offer an infinite number of solutions, some good, some bad, some new, some traditional, some feasible, and some seemingly impossible or impractical. They even present solutions that may be impossible to implement at the moment. In the creative domain, the fact that it is impossible to do is not necessarily a deterrent. Creative problem solvers must allow themselves to bridge this gap. Many innovative processes have been developed by people using creative problem techniques.

The first two types of problems are probably easier to deal with than the third. Our culture teaches us from childhood that we should conform to and use analytical and judgmental techniques to solve problems. However, when it comes to the *wild* thinking necessary for creative problem solving, our teaching and accepted patterns offer little help. It was *wild* thinking that helped us achieve most of our modern inventions and, in many cases, it remains necessary to leave behind conventional thinking to achieve results. However, when we leave normal thought patterns and try to be creative, we often encounter blocks. We need to recognize these blocks and apply techniques to remove them.

BLOCKS TO PROPER DEFINITION

Some obstacles to proper definition are external. Lack of information, lack of proper authority, and lack of knowledge about the particular problem are all common external road blocks with which everyone is familiar. However, often we are not quite as familiar with the mental attitudes which constitute internal blocks to achieving proper definition. In business and industry, these attitudes are often expressed as, "It can't be done" or "That's not my department" or some other killer phrase. Too often these killer phrases immediately shut off the creative portion of defining a problem and also affect the judgmental or analytical portions. To get around these blocks involves change, and change involves risk — the risk of failure, discomfort, or having people laugh at us. However, in problem solving we must get over these blocks and learn how to adjust to change. Too often, when members of a group are asked to reduce a *big mess* to a specific problem, their responses reflect their habitual attitudes towards their own lives, jobs, and other areas. Certainly, habitual action is necessary for smooth and efficient daily functioning. However, individuals who are never willing to think differently about anything lack the ability to change and be creative.

Mental blocks, of which we are often unaware, can be divided into three major categories — perceptual, emotional, and cultural. These blocks exist for complex and varying reasons. However, they can be overcome to some extent, depending upon our willingness to change and our ability and perseverance in analyzing them.

One of our main downfalls in the perceptual area is the inability to overcome a preconceived viewpoint or to visualize an object as having more than one function. This shortcoming may also involve the inability to see a problem in a fresh light or from another or true perspective. Those with a perceptual block try to solve a problem as they previously solved other problems, failing to differentiate between this problem, its cause and effect, and other problems. Another aspect of perceptual blocks is the inability to withhold or change immediate judgment. That is, once a judgment is made, it is made forever.

Mental blocks in the emotional area are often tied in with prejudice and closed minds. Too often we have a fear of failure, ridicule or of being different, and this fear creates anxiety, insecurity, and confusion that blocks our ability to define a problem. In our emotional domain, we are sometimes beset with a negative attitude, often a product of our environment and of our own mind. An emotionally blocked individual cannot follow another suggestion or consider another point of view.

Cultural aspects of mental blocks include apathy, complacency, and mediocrity. A culturally blocked individual places a high value on stability and is unwilling to be bothered and unwilling to change the status quo. Authority and group domination often are major factors. Personal security with the group and its leadership is more important many times to these individuals than going on their own and taking the initiative.

It takes a positive attitude to get over these blocks. Some of the keys to developing a positive attitude are:

- We must really want to take a new thrust. There must be a better way to define the problem and we must try to find it.

- We must understand and accept that we all make mistakes. It's not making the mistakes, but growing through them that is important.

- We're all on the same team. It doesn't matter who gets the credit. It only matters that the problem gets solved.

- We have no great or small people on the team, only great challenges. The group must develop a system to meet them.

- An objective-oriented group is one which shares its mistakes and its victories with each other. It considers, in the final analysis, only the fact that it is able to meet its objective, i.e., to define and eventually solve the problem.

BRAINSTORMING

Brainstorming is a primary technique in helping the group to extract the specific problem from the *big mess*.

The technique was devised by Osborne[9] during the 1930s in *Applied Imagination*. The word brainstorming has become somewhat debased over the years because it has been used to describe a group of people sitting around a table and simply throwing out ideas. These *bull sessions* usually produce a small number of ideas that are not good; as a result, this pseudo brainstorming is usually abandoned. True brainstorming, however, is different. When applied properly, it is a unique technique for identifying a specific problem at the heart of the *big mess*.

Brainstorming has been defined in many different ways but, in essence, it is a means of getting a large number of ideas creatively from a group of people in a short period of time. This definition contains three elements: (1) a large number of ideas; (2) a group of people; and (3) a short time.

Notice that the definition does not say *good ideas*, but simply ideas in large numbers. Well-run brainstorming sessions will produce hundreds of ideas. They will range from the brilliant winners to totally unacceptable, silly, and useless ideas that will be discarded. All ideas are acceptable, however. In fact, sometimes the wildest and silliest ideas will either be adopted or will prompt an idea or creative thought pattern in one of the group members that will yield the prime or best solution later on.

The second element in the definition is a group of people. It is the next important aspect in the definition. The optimum size for a brainstorming group is six to 12. In a group of this size, everyone has an opportunity to contribute ideas and there are enough people with enough differences in backgrounds, habits, culture, ideas, and knowledge to create ideas to keep the flow going. The maximum size group is 15. If a group is too large, the flow of ideas is either so great that members cannot get involved in it, or certain members feel lost and do not contribute. At the other end, members in a small group tend to be too polite and wait for others to contribute ideas. Also, undersized groups do not create the kind of synergy necessary to develop the large number of ideas we should expect from a good brainstorming session. It is also more difficult to develop a freewheeling, laughing atmosphere in a smaller group.

Many times managers say they have no time to run a brainstorming session. They simply make decisions right off the top of their heads. Yet it is possible to extract a well-defined problem from a *big mess* in a limited period of time (say 15 to 60 minutes) with a group leader in charge, a person to record the suggestions, and a group willing to confine itself to simply suggesting ideas, not discussing or arguing about them. The *absolute rule* is that there must be no criticism or judgment on any suggestions until after the session is over. Discussion or arguments are not allowed during this period. Ideas should crackle during the brainstorming session like machine-gun bullets and, when properly conducted, most people will find themselves exhausted. To ensure that a true brainstorming session occurs, the following guides are suggested:

Evaluation is ruled out. Criticism of ideas must be withheld until after the session is over. Nothing should stop the flow of information and creativity.

Freewheeling is welcome. This means letting go of the barriers or inhibitions that prevent people from dreaming and being creative. All sorts of ideas — good and bad, sensible and silly — must be allowed and recorded. The wilder the idea the better. It is easier to tame down a wild idea than to try to embellish a poor one.

Quantity is demanded. The more ideas, the greater the likelihood of having the right one. It may seem to be wrong to stress quantity at this point rather than to strive for quality. That is not true — the search for quality has not been abandoned but simply suspended until later, when judgments will be made. The group members are deliberately encouraged to produce a large quantity of ideas, regardless of quality. All ideas must be accepted.

Encourage cross-fertilization. Cross-fertilization is the process by which the ideas of one person are picked up and developed by someone else. This *hitchhiking* is extremely important in the development of new and different ideas. Participants should suggest how the ideas of others can be turned into even better ideas, or how two or more ideas which have already been suggested can be formed into still another idea. This cross-fertilization is paramount to developing good lists of brainstorming ideas. It allows the ideas to be exchanged, developed, and changed by the group under the control of the group leader.

Participation by every member of the group must be encouraged. To ensure their contribution, members are asked in rotation for their ideas and they must either offer an idea or say "pass." During actual brainstorming sessions, once the creative juices are flowing and people are becoming familiar with each other, the rotation process can be suspended.

The most important argument in favor of the brainstorming technique is that it works when it is properly controlled. In addition, almost any group of people can learn quickly to think up scores of ideas for most problems. Other successful techniques can be used, but brainstorming has been one of the most common and most effective methods.

DEFINITION PROCEDURE FOR DISTIL

While the DISTIL definition step uses classic brainstorming as its main thrust, it also contains other elements to make it much more effective as a defining process. In order to ensure maximum involvement and output, it is often necessary to *prime* a group. *Priming* is accomplished by a technique known as brainwriting. Here's how it works: The group decides on the problem to be defined and then each individual is asked to create a personal list of both good and bad ideas. Generally these ideas are created on a small slip of paper and, at certain time intervals, the papers are exchanged. One person reads what someone else has written and then spends some time adding new ideas to the other person's list. This process is repeated over and over again until the total brainwriting period is completed. Then the finished sheet is returned to the original owner. Not only has this created the nucleus of many ideas, but it also ensures that each person has about ten good definitive ideas for the upcoming group brainstorming session. This almost totally removes the possibility that some people will not be involved because, even if they have not created many ideas themselves, they have ideas and sugggestions created by other people on their individual sheets.

At this point the group brainstorming session begins. The general rules previously discussed should be followed. It is important that the group leader be skilled and trained in handling the group — keeping the group moving and the ideas flowing. Even if the creative well tends to run dry, the leader must not allow the group to stop. He must probe them in various ways, using various techniques to keep the brainstorming going until a large number of ideas have been placed on the sheets. Every idea must be recorded. Every idea should also be numbered as it is placed on the group brainstorming list. These numbers will allow for easy access and identification later when the selection process begins. As a general rule of thumb, a brainstorming session must not be completed during one meeting of the group. Some time should be left between the accumulation of a large quantity of ideas and discussion of them. This technique allows for what is known as deferred ideation — the deferring of discussion of ideas until a later date. During the deferral period, people will often suggest new ideas that can then be added to the brainstorming list before discussion occurs.

It is imperative that the group talk about each idea before any type of selection process. Too often this discussion phase is rushed through and not enough time is spent on the silly or way-out ideas. Caution should be taken because it is important to discuss these! They should not be discarded until they have been thoroughly examined and understood. Once discussion of the entire brainstorming list has been completed, the top ideas for further discussion and analysis should be selected. Consensus voting techniques are used to accomplish this. To begin, the entire group votes on the ideas suggested. The number of votes received by each idea should be visibly placed on the sheet using a different color pencil or pen so they can readily be seen and understood by the group. Once an idea has been presented and placed on the brainstorming chart, it no longer belongs to the individual; it becomes the group's idea.

Once the consensus voting has been completed, the top six to 10 ideas should be selected and discussed further. This can take as long as necessary to satisfy the needs of the group. Once the discussion is finished, the major topics should be ranked by using other methods. The group must now determine the characteristics or categories that will allow them to put their ideas into proper perspective. These categories may include the ability to solve a problem, the length of time to solve a problem, the cost, probability of success, impact on quality, etc. For many groups, the task of categorizing ideas and putting them into perspective can be completed during a discussion period. Sometimes if a group is made up of various authority levels in the organization, discussion alone is not enough. At this point an affinity analysis is often appropriate.

Affinity analysis provides a group or team with a nonverbal participative method that sorts and arranges items in order of priority. Affinity analysis is used:

1. To acknowledge the facts. When facts and assumptions about a situation are in the *big mess* arena, affinity analysis provides a systematic sorting technique.

2. To build the philosophy. When a team is in a chaotic situation, affinity analysis can be used to arrange them into an orderly pattern.

3. To break away from the present situation. When traditional concepts and killer phrases as discussed previously, are blocking a team's progress, affinity analysis can aid in producing new ideas.

4. To foster participation. When different types of people from different levels of the organization are functioning as a team, affinity analysis can provide a nonverbal way for positive interaction and group dynamics.

Affinity analysis is conducted in the following way:

The group decides on the characteristics that are to be used in the priority process. The team selects the top four or five categories, such as types of problems, time to implement, cost, probability of success, etc. The ideas are transferred to idea cards, such as those shown in figure 3.1, which contain the evaluation matrix. Header cards indicating high, medium, or low priority are placed on the table, and the team, without discussion, separates the cards into one of the given levels. Silent interaction is continued until team consensus is achieved. The ratings are converted to a numeric scale and placed on the card under the appropriate headings after all categories have been evaluated. The overall impact of a particular idea then can be calculated.

QUALITY TECHNICS
TAPS

IDEA: (Keyword)

Explanation:

By:

TAPS PRIORITY INDEX					
Type	Time	Cost	Success	Quality	Total
Individual Problem		Assigned To:			
		Controlled By:			

Figure 3.1 TAPS affinity analysis card.

If left entirely to their own devices, many groups would evaluate ideas in a haphazard fashion relying on their intuitive guesses. To reduce the risk of failure in this phase, the affinity analysis procedure was created. It allows not only for evaluation and interaction, but also creates a nonthreatening atmosphere for people who do not feel comfortable using their oral skills. The results of the affinity analysis can be used to develop an evaluation grid for priority indexing. Figure 3.2 shows an affinity analysis chart.

EVALUATION CHART

PROBLEMS LIST	CRITERIA *								YOUR TOTAL	TEAM TOTAL
1.										
2.										
3.										
4.										
5.										
6.										
7.										
8.										
9.										
10.										
11.										
12.										
13.										
14.										

*USE: 1-Good, Easy, Short; 2-Average; 3-Poor, Hard, Long

Figure 3.2   Affinity analysis chart.

The group has now converted their ideas into definitive numbers and has moved from a creative atmosphere in an initial brainstorming step to a logical or analytical phase. It is usually a simple task for the group to identify that one particular problem which will define their task and focus their efforts.

Through team consensus, the group has reduced the general problem area to one specific problem, but now they need to put it precisely in a simple statement of the problem. Through discussion the team must decide on its wording, using these guidelines:

- Start with the word "to" followed by an action verb. This is the cause.

- Specify a simple key result, avoiding excessive verbiage. This then becomes the effect.

- An example is: *Cause* — to weld a part so it is flawless. *Effect* — flawless weld.

- Another example: *Cause* — to bake a cake so it is delicious. *Effect* — delicious cake.

This statement may need to be redefined many times during the group session. It is important to make the statement and put it into a visual form which can be displayed.

CASE EXAMPLES

To help understand the DISTIL concept, we will show step-by-step two case examples, one in manufacturing and one in the services.

MANUFACTURING — RAL CHEMICAL CORPORATION

BACKGROUND

This team consists of nine members:

- Manufacturing manager

- Process engineer (leader)

- Two shift supervisors

- Four operators

- Plant engineer

RAL is a three-shift, specialty chemical, batch-processing operation. Their first step was to define the problem by reducing the many problems down to one that was important and would significantly improve the situation if corrected. They used brainstorming to accomplish this step. Part of the team's list was as follows:

Initial Brainstorming — RAL's Manufacturing Problems

1. Erratic preventive maintenance

2. Late orders to floor

3. Raw materials not available

4. Low yields

5. Incorrect standards

6. Poor lighting

7. Illegible handwriting

8. Misunderstandings between shifts

9. Insufficient backshift supervision

10. Insufficient backshift support, expertise

11. Frequent equipment breakdowns

12. Confusing instructions

13. High reject rates for the preform operation and weights

14. Poorly trained part-time and summer help

15. Old equipment

16. Malfunctioning controllers

17. Lack of calibration

18. Too much "accept as is"

19. High humidity and temperature

20. Incomplete production orders

21. Dirty conditions

22. Mislabeling

This list was then narrowed to six important problems through consensus voting. The votes are tallied in parenthesis after the problem.

Consensus Vote — Initial Brainstorming

1. Erratic preventive maintenance (2)

2. Late orders to floor (1)

3. Raw materials not available (6)

4. Low yields (4)

5. Incorrect standards (6)

6. Poor lighting (8)

7. Illegible handwriting (2)

8. Misunderstandings between shifts (3)

9. Insufficient backshift supervision (8)

10. Insufficient backshift support, expertise (5)

11. Frequent equipment breakdowns (5)

12. Confusing instructions (8)

13. High reject rates for the preform operation and weights (9)

14. Poorly trained part-time and summer help (7)

15. Old equipment (0)

16. Malfunctioning controllers (4)

17. Lack of calibration (6)

18. Too much "accept as is" (9)

19. High humidity and temperature (3)

20. Incomplete production orders (9)

21. Dirty conditions (2)

22. Mislabeling (4)

From this partial list the consensus vote narrowed the problems down to the top six (those with eight or nine votes).

Affinity Analysis, Top Problems

Next the team brainstormed, discussed, and voted on the characteristics to use in evaluating the problems. They were:

1. Political acceptance (3)

2. Time to solve problem (9)

3. Is it legal? (0)

4. Probability of solving successfully (8)

5. Impact on quality (9)

6. Cost to solve or correct (8)

7. Type of problem to solve (8)

8. Impact on manufacturing if corrected (2)

The characteristics chosen to evaluate the problems are shown in the evaluation chart (Figure 3.3). Figure 3.4 shows the same evaluation chart, but includes the way one individual voted on each characteristic for each problem. The next step in the definition-reduction process was to sum up all the team members' votes for each problem. This is shown in Figure 3.5.

EVALUATION CHART

RAL CHEMICAL CORP. PROBLEMS LIST	TIME	SUCCESS	QUALITY	CRITERIA * COST	TYPE			YOUR TOTAL	TEAM TOTAL
1. POOR LIGHTING									
2. INSUFFICIENT BACKSHIFT SUPERVISION									
3. CONFUSING INSTRUCTIONS									
4. HIGH REJECT RATES, PREFORM WEIGHTS									
5. TOO MUCH "ACCEPT AS IS"									
6. INCOMPLETE PRODUCTION ORDERS									
7.									
8.									
9.									
10.									
11.									
12.									
13.									
14.									

*USE: 1-Good, Easy, Short; 2-Average; 3-Poor, Hard, Long

Figure 3.3 Characteristics chosen to evaluate the problems at RAL Chemical Corporation.

EVALUATION CHART

RAL CHEMICAL CORP. PROBLEMS LIST	TIME	SUCCESS	QUALITY	COST	TYPE	CRITERIA *			YOUR TOTAL	TEAM TOTAL
1. POOR LIGHTING	1	2	2	3	1				9	
2. INSUFFICIENT BACKSHIFT SUPERVISION	2	2	2	3	3				12	
3. CONFUSING INSTRUCTIONS	1	2	1	2	1				7	
4. HIGH REJECT RATES, PREFORM WEIGHTS	1	1	1	2	2				7	
5. TOO MUCH "ACCEPT AS IS"	2	1	1	1	3				8	
6. INCOMPLETE PRODUCTION ORDERS	1	1	1	2	1				6	
7.										
8.										
9.										
10.										
11.										
12.										
13.										
14.										

*USE: 1-Good, Easy, Short; 2-Average; 3-Poor, Hard, Long

Figure 3.4 Same as Figure 3.3 showing how one individual voted on each characteristic for each problem.

EVALUATION CHART

RAL CHEMICAL CORP. PROBLEMS LIST	TIME	SUCCESS	QUALITY	COST	TYPE	CRITERIA *			YOUR TOTAL	TEAM TOTAL
1. POOR LIGHTING	1	2	2	3	1				9	80
2. INSUFFICIENT BACKSHIFT SUPERVISION	2	2	2	3	3				12	100
3. CONFUSING INSTRUCTIONS	1	2	1	2	1				7	60
4. HIGH REJECT RATES, PREFORM WEIGHTS	1	1	1	2	2				7	52
5. TOO MUCH "ACCEPT AS IS"	2	1	1	1	3				8	75
6. INCOMPLETE PRODUCTION ORDERS	1	1	1	2	1				6	56
7.										
8.										
9.										
10.										
11.										
12.										
13.										
14.										

*USE: 1-Good, Easy, Short; 2-Average; 3-Poor, Hard, Long

Figure 3.5 Same as Figure 3.3 showing the sum of all the team members' votes for each problem.

The final step was to take the one problem (lowest total value) and make it a problem statement. This team's problem was to reduce the out-of-weight specification preforms. The team was ready to image this problem (effect) as seen in Chapter 4.

CASE EXAMPLES

SERVICE — JAM INSURANCE COMPANY

BACKGROUND

The eight-member team was made up of the following data processing personnel:

- Manager (leader)

- Development programmer

- Two data entry operators

- Analyst

- Maintenance programmer

- Two computer operators

JAM is a medium-sized insurance company.

The teams brainstormed the general topic *department problems*, with the goal of identifying one significant problem to correct. The partial list of problems brought up during initial brainstorming include:

JAM Data Processing Problems

1. Response time or throughput time

2. External data not received on time

3. Policy entry errors

4. Illegible handwriting on orders

5. Hardware breakdowns

6. Poorly programmed systems

7. Poorly designed development programs

8. Inadequate user training

9. Lack of control of personal computers

10. Poor documentation

11. Keeping current with hardware and software technology

12. Keeping personnel current on technology

13. Incompatible upgrading

14. Turnover in personnel

15. Interruptions

16. Software or program errors

17. Poor documentation on purchased software

18. Communication with people who are not computer literate

19. Poor communication between departments

20. Insufficient or incorrect information on incoming documents

21. Personality clashes

After discussing these, the team narrowed the list through consensus voting. The tallies are indicated in parentheses after the problem.

Consenus Vote — Initial Brainstorming

1. Response time or throughput time (5)

2. External data not received on time (7)

3. Policy entry errors (8)

4. Illegible handwriting on orders (5)

5. Hardware breakdowns (3)

6. Poorly programmed systems (5)

7. Poorly designed development programs (6)

8. Inadequate user training (6)

9. Lack of control of personal computers (3)

10. Poor documentation (8)

11. Keeping current with hardware and software technology (3)

12. Keeping personnel current on technology (6)

13. Incompatible upgrading (1)

14. Turnover in personnel (4)

15. Interruptions (6)

16. Software or program errors (2)

17. Poor documentation on purchased software (1)

18. Communication with people who are not computer literate (3)

19. Poor communication between departments (8)

20. Insufficient or incorrect information on incoming documents (7)

21. Personality clashes (0)

The voting narrowed the problems to the top five (those with seven or eight votes).

Affinity Analysis — Top Problems

Next the team brainstormed, then discussed and voted (in parentheses) on characteristics to use in evaluating the problems:

1. Success — probability of solving problem (8)

2. Cost to correct (8)

3. Is it legal? (1)

4. Time to solve (7)

5. Impact on quality (8)

6. Impact on data processing if corrected (8)

7. Type of problem to solve (7)

8. Acceptance by people involved (2)

The characteristics chosen to evaluate the problems are shown in the evaluation chart (Figure 3.6). Figure 3.7 shows the same evaluation chart after adding the way one individual voted. The sum of all the team members' votes is shown in Figure 3.8.

The final step of the definition phase was to take one problem (lowest vote total) and make it a problem statement. The problem was: to reduce policy entry errors. The team was now ready to image this problem (effect).

EVALUATION CHART

JAM INSURANCE PROBLEMS LIST	SUCCESS	CRITERIA * COST	TIME	QUALITY	IMPACT	TYPE		YOUR TOTAL	TEAM TOTAL
1. External Data Not Received On Time									
2. Policy Entry Errors									
3. Poor Documentation									
4. Poor Communication Between Departments									
5. Insufficient or Incorrect Information on Incoming Documents									
6.									
7.									
8.									
9.									
10.									
11.									
12.									
13.									
14.									

*USE: 1-Good, Easy, Short; 2-Average; 3-Poor, Hard, Long

Figure 3.6 Characteristics chosen to evaluate the problems at JAM Insurance Company.

EVALUATION CHART

| JAM INSURANCE PROBLEMS LIST | SUCCESS | CRITERIA * | | | | | | YOUR TOTAL | TEAM TOTAL |
		COST	TIME	QUALITY	IMPACT	TYPE			
1. External Data Not Received On Time	2	1	3	1	1	3		11	
2. Policy Entry Errors	1	1	2	1	1	2		8	
3. Poor Documentation	3	1	3	1	2	3		13	
4. Poor Communication Between Departments	2	1	2	2	1	2		10	
5. Insufficient or Incorrect Information on Incoming Documents	3	2	2	1	2	2		12	
6.									
7.									
8.									
9.									
10.									
11.									
12.									
13.									
14.									

*USE: 1-Good, Easy, Short; 2-Average; 3-Poor, Hard, Long

Figure 3.7   Same as Figure 3.6 showing how one individual voted on each characteristic for each problem.

EVALUATION CHART

| JAM INSURANCE PROBLEMS LIST | SUCCESS | CRITERIA * | | | | | | YOUR TOTAL | TEAM TOTAL |
		COST	TIME	QUALITY	IMPACT	TYPE			
1. External Data Not Received On Time	2	1	3	1	1	3		11	86
2. Policy Entry Errors	1	1	2	1	1	2		8	68
3. Poor Documentation	3	1	3	1	2	3		13	116
4. Poor Communication Between Departments	2	1	2	2	1	2		10	96
5. Insufficient or Incorrect Information on Incoming Documents	3	2	2	1	2	2		12	110
6.									
7.									
8.									
9.									
10.									
11.									
12.									
13.									
14.									

*USE: 1-Good, Easy, Short; 2-Average; 3-Poor, Hard, Long

Figure 3.8   Same as Figure 3.6 showing the sum of all the team members' votes for each problem.

4
IMAGE

Man has an imagination which must be used and enjoyed in order for him to experience the complete fulfillment of life.

George Eckstein

GENERAL

The "I" in DISTIL stands for image. It is the second step in problem solving. We have a definition of our effect from the first step of our problem-solving process. Now, having defined that effect, we must image it to visually see what we are working on.

What's the best way to image or visualize the problem or effect we are working on? We believe it is through the use of a cause-and-effect diagram or cause and effect. Cause and effect help us to visualize or image the problem and its causes.

While structured problem-solving techniques have been around a long time, the particular format known as cause and effect analysis was developed and named by Professor Kaoru Ishikawa of the University of Tokyo in 1950. They are also known as Ishikawa Diagrams or Ishikawa Fishbone Diagrams. Professor Ishikawa developed this tool as a means of teaching the concept of control for processes containing many factors and characteristics. He made his first application in the workshop at Fukii Iron Works, Tokyo, in 1953, where the technique proved its effectiveness. Since that time its application has become widely known.

The cause-and-effect diagram is a picture composed of lines and symbols designed to represent a meaningful relationship between the effect and its causes. The cause-and-effect diagram helps us to portray pictorially situations which are so complex that they are difficult to explain and understand using words alone. They have been created to portray a rather specific set of purposes. For every effect there are likely to be many interrelated causes. A *cause enumeration* cause-and-effect diagram is shown in Figure 4.1.

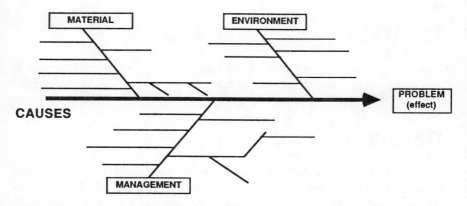

Figure 4.1   Cause-and-effect diagram.

This diagram is constructed in the following manner, using a six-step process:

Step 1 — Identify problem. From our first step in DISTIL (the D), we have identified and defined our effect. Therefore, begin by writing the problem on the right hand side and draw an arrow pointing to it (Figure 4.2).

Figure 4.2   Arrow drawn pointing to problem.

Step 2 — Categorize major causes. We need next to determine the major types of causes that other possible causes could be grouped under. A good way to start is to use the four "M's" (man, material, method, and machine). If the four "M's" are not appropriate, don't use them. There are many choices; the starting choices for the major causes should be brainstormed by the team. The number of major causes can vary. It can be as many as six or as few as one. Numbers beyond six should probably be broken into more than one cause-and-effect diagram (Figure 4.3).

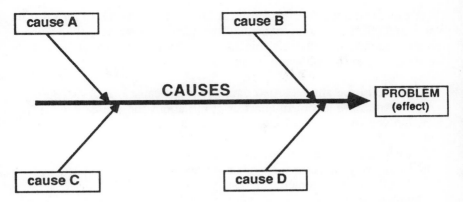

Figure 4.3 Cause-and-effect diagram showing more than one cause.

Step 3 — Brainstorming. Now that we have the major causes as brainstormed by the group or through consensus, we start getting subcauses. The first round consists of asking each member of the group to suggest a possible cause for our effect. This is then added to the branch of the cause-and-effect diagram. If there is concern about where to put a sub-cause, just put it under any major one (no need to get hung up on where it belongs). We suggest using Post-it-Notes (Commercial Tape Division/3M, St. Paul, Minn.) for attaching the causes to the cause-and-effect diagrams. That way you can change them around as well as let others participate if you so desire.

After going around once, ask the team to individually brainwrite the five causes that they can think of. This gives individuals a chance to think of some new ideas before continuing, after the seeds of the first round have been planted. After they have written their five ideas, go around the team again, asking them to attach their causes to the cause-and-effect diagram. If there are duplicate ideas, don't worry. Keep them together or note them. This continues until all causes have been exhausted. Then continue with open brainstorming until you have covered all the causes mentioned. At this point, we suggest allowing some time for these causes to set in your mind — take a break or continue the process on another day. Figure 4.4 illustrates how a typical cause-and-effect diagram might look.

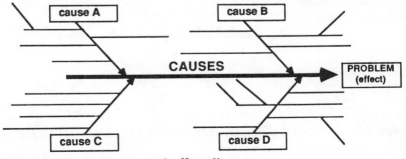

Figure 4.4 Typical cause-and-effect diagram.

Step 4 — Data gathering. Ishikawa, in his original procedure for creating cause and effect diagrams, suggested that extensive data be gathered about possible causes. In gathering this data, Ishikawa suggests that each cause be subjected to the following questions:

1. Do you have any recorded data about the cause? (RC)
2. Do you have a control chart or graph about the cause? (CC) (G)
3. Do you regulate the factor everyday? (RG)
4. Has the factor been standardized? (ST)
5. Is the factor a variable or attribute? (VF) (AF)
6. Is the factor a factor for bias or precision? (B) (P)
7. Are there any interactions? (I)

The symbols are added to the cause-and-effect diagram as appropriate. In some cases the data will strongly suggest the most probable causes. In other cases, it will be a factor to be used by the team during consensus voting. In all cases the final accepted most probable causes should be selected by the team using consensus voting.

Step 5 — Most likely causes. After all the causes have been listed, the data gathered, and the cause-and-effect diagram has set for a short period of time, the team should critically analyze the causes and identify the most likely true causes. It should be noted that there is another advantage to the waiting period: members of the group are less likely to remember who suggested any particular cause. It is therefore much easier to criticize the ideas and not the person who suggested them. There should be, at this point, an open discussion on all causes that need clarification or that anybody might want to critique. After this process, establish the most probable true causes by consensus vote. This would be voting on each cause but not voting against any cause. None of the suggestions is erased even if it isn't given any votes. The top vote-getters are circled as probable true causes. The group will have to turn back to the cause-and-effect diagram for further analysis (Figure 4.5).

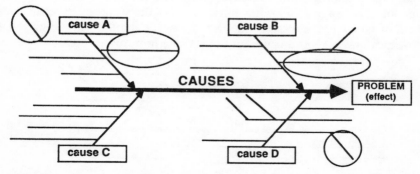

Figure 4.5   Cause-and-effect diagram showing the causes getting the most votes circled.

Step 6 — Most likely cause. We must now reduce the number of probably true causes to the most likely cause. This step moves us into the "S" in DISTIL, the selection process which will be discussed in Chapter 5.

CASE EXAMPLES

MANUFACTURING — RAL CHEMICAL CORPORATION

The team defined the problem as addressing the out-of-weight specification preforms, and used cause-and-effect diagramming to move on to the imaging phase. They started with a basic cause-and-effect diagram (Figure 4.6) using the 4 Ms to brainstorm for causes.

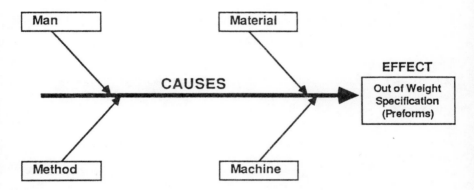

Figure 4.6   Cause-and-effect diagram for RAL Chemical Corporation.

The possible causes the team came up with for out-of-specification preforms are shown in Figure 4.7. These causes were the result of initial brainstorming and, allowing for a waiting period of several days, followup.

The possible causes were discussed. The team then voted to identify the most probable causes. Figure 4.8 shows the results of the voting, with the most probable causes circled. In order to determine the most likely cause, the team moved into the selection phase (Chapter 5).

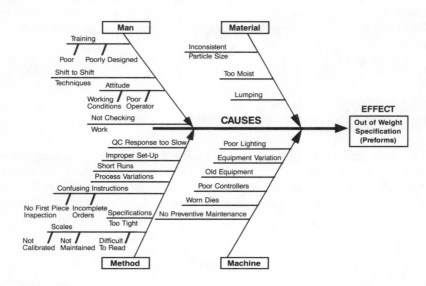

Figure 4.7 Possible causes for out-of-specification preforms for RAL Chemical Corporation.

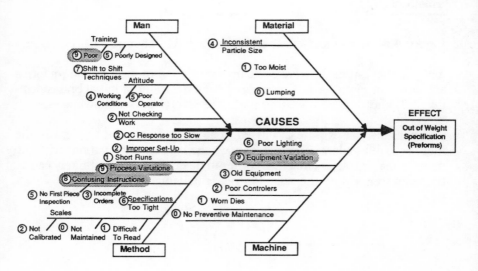

Figure 4.8 Causes voted to be most probable for out-of-specification preforms for RAL Chemical Corporation.

SERVICE — JAM INSURANCE COMPANY

The team's problem was to reduce policy entry errors. They then moved into the imaging phase where cause-and-effect diagramming was used. The basic diagram is shown in Figure 4.9. They used three major headings to identify the possible causes. After an hour of brainstorming and finishing a day later, the results were listed (Figure 4.10).

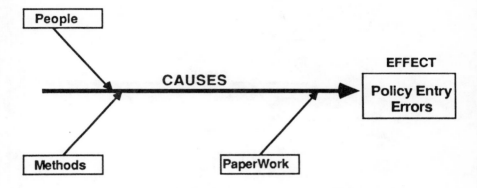

Figure 4.9 Cause-and-effect diagram for Jam Insurance Company for reducing policy entry errors.

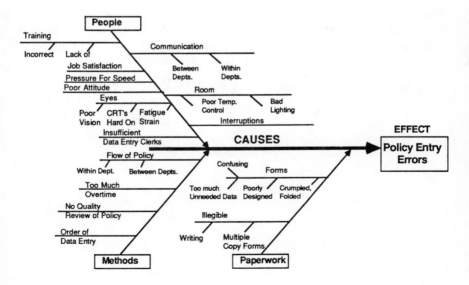

Figure 4.10 Possible causes for policy entry errors for JAM Insurance Company.

After discussing these causes, the team decided to use consensus voting to reduce the many causes to a few most likely causes. The results of the voting, with the most likely circled, are shown in Figure 4.11.

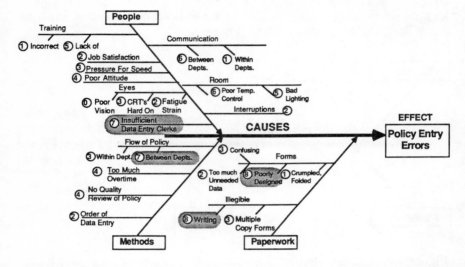

Figure 4.11   Shows causes voted to be most likely for policy entry errors for JAM Insurance Company.

After agreement on the most likely causes, the team now needed to select the one most likely cause. The next step, the selection phase, is discussed in Chapter 5.

5
SELECTION

Selection Process — A structured method to achieve consensus acceptance to the proposed solution that has the best potential to solve the specific problem.

L. N. Jones

GENERAL

The "S" in DISTIL stands for selection. This is the third step in the problem-solving process. Now that we have imaged our problem and seen what it looks like through cause-and-effect diagramming, we are ready to select a most likely cause.

The selection process has two phases. The first involves selecting the most probable cause; the second the best solution. In order to remove some of the subjectivity in selecting the most probable cause, we use a priority ranking system. Often in team settings and especially with new teams or those inadequately developed, some individuals, frequently the leader, are strongly influential. This bias must be minimized so that everyone on the team is heard and has an equal part in the decision-making process. By using an individual ranking system, team members express their opinion with minimal influence.

To illustrate this potential influence, we recall the situation with a new team formed with limited training and team development. When they got to selecting the most probable cause, they discussed the top contenders and verbally voted on the top one. It didn't take a trained observer to see which one would win: The team leader, a strong-willed person, made it clear which one he thought was the most likely. The voice vote was merely a show. Everyone knew which would get the most votes. This greatly reduced the team's effectiveness, didn't allow for open, objective discussions, and set the tone for the team's future sessions.

While the individual ranking system cannot assure the individual will not be overly influenced by one person, it does give the team members the opportunity to express themselves.

First, individually rank in order of priority each of the top most probable causes. This is done without discussion, based on personal preferences. Figure 5.1 shows a simple format that can be used.

INDIVIDUAL RANKING

RANK	PROBABLE CAUSES - KEYWORDS
1.	
2.	
3.	
4.	
5.	
6.	
7.	
8.	

Figure 5.1 Simple format used for ranking in order of priority each of the top most probable causes for individuals.

Once everyone has completed individual rankings, the individual values must be combined to give a composite team ranking. This is simply a compilation of the individual rankings and can be done on a flip chart or overhead using a simple format (Figure 5.2).

TEAM RANKINGS

PROBABLE CAUSES - KEYWORDS	RANKING								TOTAL
	1.	2.	3.	4.	5.	6.	7.	8.	
A.									
B.									
C.									
D.									
E.									
F.									
G.									
H.									

Figure 5.2 Same as Figure 5.1 for team.

With the team's compiled data, the most probable cause should be readily identified. It will be the one with the lowest total, indicating it received the highest ranking by the most individuals. This most probable cause is the one the team identified and selected to solve their problem. However, this is a cause, not a solution. There are generally many options for correcting it.

We now must determine the best solution for the most probable cause. The best solution will come from a list of probable solutions that is generated by the team. Generally, several options should be discussed. These solutions can be evaluated using a format such as that shown in Figure 5.3.

SOLUTION SELECTION CHART

MOST PROBABLE CAUSE - _____

POSSIBLE SOLUTIONS	Fixes The Root Cause (Yes/No)	Creates New Problems (Yes/No)	Management Receptivity (Yes/No)	Group Can Implement (Yes/No)	Cost (High/Low)

Figure 5.3   Format for evaluating possible solutions.

By taking each potential solution and asking questions such as Does this solution create new problems?, the best solution begins to surface — one that goes to the root cause and best fits the situation. The best solution should reflect the consensus of the team. Testing it to ensure its validity is the next step of our DISTIL problem-solving process.

CASE EXAMPLES

MANUFACTURING — RAL CHEMICAL CORPORATION

With four most probable causes from the team's imaging, the next step was to use cause-and-effect analysis to select the most likely cause. A simple ranking procedure is used to accomplish this. Each team member ranked the four causes from 1 to 4 (the most likely to the least). Figure 5.4 shows how one individual ranked them.

RAL CHEMICAL

INDIVIDUAL RANKING - John McBee

RANK	PROBABLE CAUSES - KEYWORDS
1.	PROCESS VARIATION
2.	EQUIPMENT VARIATION
3.	POOR TRAINING
4.	CONFUSING INSTRUCTIONS
5.	
6.	
7.	
8.	

Figure 5.4 Individual ranking for possible causes for RAL Chemical Corporation.

After all team members individually ranked the results, they were compiled for the team. Figure 5.5 illustrates the team's tabulation. The total is a sum of the number of members ranking a particular cause times the ranking. The cause with the lowest total is the one the team believes to be the most likely cause of the effect. This probable cause had more than one solution (Figure 5.6).

RAL CHEMICAL

TEAM RANKINGS - Production Team

| PROBABLE CAUSES - KEYWORDS | RANKING | | | | | | | | |
	1.	2.	3.	4.	5.	6.	7.	8.	TOTAL
A. POOR TRAINING	1	2	4	2					25
B. PROCESS VARIATION	5	3	1	0					14
C. EQUIPMENT VARIATION	3	3	1	2					20
D. CONFUSING INSTRUCTIONS	0	1	3	5					32
E.									
F.									
G.									
H.									

Figure 5.5 Team ranking for probable causes.

SOLUTION SELECTION CHART

RAL CHEMICAL

MOST PROBABLE CAUSE - PROCESS VARIATION

POSSIBLE SOLUTIONS	Fixes The Root Cause (Yes/No)	Creates New Problems (Yes/No)	Management Receptivity (Yes/No)	Group Can Implement (Yes/No)	Cost (High/Low)
AUTOMATIC CONTROLLERS					
STATISTICAL PROCESS CONTROL					
MORE SUPERVISION					
MORE INSPECTION BY QC					
TIGHTER SPECIFICATION LIMITS					

Figure 5.6   Solution selection chart for probable causes.

The various solutions were discussed in several team meetings and a consensus was reached on each of the five critical questions. The final results are shown in Figure 5.7.

SOLUTION SELECTION CHART

RAL CHEMICAL

MOST PROBABLE CAUSE - PROCESS VARIATION

POSSIBLE SOLUTIONS	Fixes The Root Cause (Yes/No)	Creates New Problems (Yes/No)	Management Receptivity (Yes/No)	Group Can Implement (Yes/No)	Cost (High/Low)
AUTOMATIC CONTROLLERS	YES	YES	YES	YES	HIGH
STATISTICAL PROCESS CONTROL	YES	NO	YES	YES	LOW
MORE SUPERVISION	NO	NO	NO	YES	HIGH
MORE INSPECTION BY QC	NO	NO	YES	YES	LOW
TIGHTER SPECIFICATION LIMITS	NO	YES	NO	YES	LOW

Figure 5.7   Find results for most probable cause.

From the selection chart, the team agreed that a statistical process control solution was best. The next phase (discussed in Chapter 6) questioned if it could be tested and measured.

SERVICE — JAM INSURANCE COMPANY

From the cause-and-effect analysis, the team yielded four most likely causes for policy entry errors. To decide which one was the most probable cause they used a ranking system. Each member ranked the four causes from 1 to 4 (the most likely cause to the least). Figure 5.8 indicates how one person ranked the most likely causes.

JAM INSURANCE

INDIVIDUAL RANKING - D. Long

RANK	PROBABLE CAUSES - KEYWORDS
1.	POORLY DESIGNED FORMS
2.	WRITING ILLEGIBLE
3.	INSUFFICIENT DATA ENTRY CLERKS
4.	BETWEEN DEPTS, POLICY FLOW
5.	
6.	
7.	
8.	

Figure 5.8 Individual ranking for probable causes for JAM Insurance Company.

After all the members completed their individual rankings, the results were compiled for the team. Figure 5.9 illustrates the team's summary. The total is a sum of the number of members ranking a particular cause times the ranking. The cause with the lowest total is the one the team felt was the most likely cause of the effect.

JAM INSURANCE

TEAM RANKINGS

PROBABLE CAUSES - KEYWORDS	RANKING								TOTAL
	1.	2.	3.	4.	5.	6.	7.	8.	
A. INSUFFICIENT CLERKS	0	2	2	4					26
B. FLOW-BETWEEN DEPARTMENTS	2	4	1	1					17
C. POORLY DESIGNED FORMS	6	1	1	0					11
D. WRITING ILLEGIBLE	0	1	4	3					25
E.									
F.									
G.									
H.									

Figure 5.9   Team ranking for probable causes.

Like most solutions, the team identified and discussed several possibilities. Figure 5.10 shows the results of their discussions. From the selection chart, the team decided by consensus that the best solution was to redesign the forms. This is shown in Figure 5.11. The next phase (Chapter 6) questioned if the solution could be tested and measured.

SOLUTION SELECTION CHART

JAM INSURANCE

MOST PROBABLE CAUSE - POORLY DESIGNED FORMS

POSSIBLE SOLUTIONS	Fixes The Root Cause (Yes/No)	Creates New Problems (Yes/No)	Management Receptivity (Yes/No)	Group Can Implement (Yes/No)	Cost (High/Low)
REDESIGN, INTERNALLY					
REDESIGN, USE CONSULTANTS					
BUY STANDARD FORMS					
ELIMINATE FORMS					

Figure 5.10   Solution selection chart for probable causes.

SOLUTION SELECTION CHART

JAM INSURANCE

MOST PROBABLE CAUSE - POORLY DESIGNED FORMS

POSSIBLE SOLUTIONS	Fixes The Root Cause (Yes/No)	Creates New Problems (Yes/No)	Management Receptivity (Yes/No)	Group Can Implement (Yes/No)	Cost (High/Low)
REDESIGN, INTERNALLY	YES	NO	YES	YES	LOW
REDESIGN, USE CONSULTANTS	YES	NO	NO	NO	HIGH
BUY STANDARD FORMS	?	?	NO	YES	HIGH
ELIMINATE FORMS	NO	YES	NO	YES	LOW

Figure 5.11 Fixed results for most probable cause.

6
TEST

Anything worth doing is worth doing small.

Tom Smith, Insight Research

GENERAL

Once a solution is agreed upon by the team there is a strong tendency to move rapidly into the implementation stage. This need for immediate and decisive action is especially strong in American industries where short-term gains and payback are strong criteria for supporting and sponsoring problem-solving teams.

This is, however, the stage where the group must pause, take a deep team breath, and contemplate questions such as:

- Can we test the selected best solution? Can it be tested experimentally or in its actual full-scale setting?

- What statistic or other data are required to test the solution?

- Can knowledge obtained during the test stage be used to ensure or increase the probability of successful full-scale implementation?

Time spent determining the answers to these questions will enable the team to work smarter, rather than harder. If you think too big at this stage, you drastically reduce your chances of success. What may seem like an ideal solution to your team will seem useless to many and a definite threat to others. Those against your solution will seize potential big impacts — high cost, interruption of the present system, etc. — as excuses to delay or defeat it. By testing on a small scale you give yourself the option to move forward a step at a time, while making corrections and adjustments as required. This testing step is subdivided into three parts, i.e., goal setting, data gathering, and test monitoring.

TESTING SOLUTION AGAINST GOAL

A goal can be defined as what we want or expect at some time in the future, including the contribution we make by reaching the goal. It would be ideal if a satisfactory goal statement could be created and accepted by the team early in the process, but too often we don't know enough. Even if an acceptable goal statement has been created, it should be studied and possibly revised as the first phase of the test step.

The following steps should be used in creating a goal statement:

1. Start with the word "to" followed by an action verb.

2. Specify a single key result to be accomplished. It should answer a question starting with "what."

3. Specify a measure of accomplishment that answers the question, "how much" or "how long."

4. Specify a target date for accomplishment.

5. Specify maximum cost factors, if possible.

6. Specify results, not activities. Ask "why" of the goal at least three times.

7. Avoid excess verbiage (KISS principle).

8. Make certain that each goal is realistic, attainable, and challenging.

Setting goals is not a one-time activity. Goals need to be monitored and updated as information is received, compiled, and correlated. For example, the pretesting goal may indicate the solution will be implemented using existing equipment, but data gathered during the testing might indicate that present equipment is incapable of achieving the desired results. This information and its implication should be factored into a revised goal statement. Thus, the final goal statement provides a vehicle by which the fully implemented solution can be evaluated and judged.

TEST MONITORING

SPC and other statistical methods should be applied in gathering and properly evaluating test data. Because SPC is a technique which uses statistics to monitor the consistency of a process, it can provide important information about assignable or inherent variation. By eliminating assignable causes during the testing phase, the process can not only be observed when a constant-cause system exists, but this system also can provide valuable insight during scale-up and into full-scale production. Control limits that indicate the maximum expected variation during test phases can provide tentative control limits for the actual process.

Because controlling variables is often easier during prototype testing, this is an appropriate time to ascertain the process capability indices. This information can be used by knowledgeable personnel to establish tolerances and specifications which will satisfy both customer and producer.

Other more exotic statistical techniques such as correlation analysis, analysis of variance (ANOVA), and evalutionary operation (EVOP) can often be applied during the test stage at minimal expense. Insight gained at this stage can yield immediate improvements and allow for long-term prediction about the effect and impact of the selected solutions.

The test phase is one of risk taking. Do not be afraid of rejecting your selected solution if evidence indicates high probability of failure.

Return to the solution selection matrix and reevaluate other possible solutions. This phase is also one of opportunity. Take this time to identify all people affected by the implementation. Keep them informed and, if possible, get them involved so they can "buy into" the solution early. This is also the time to develop a strategy for resolving resistance from negative factions. Determine the people who can be key resources to aid in implementation and final acceptance. They will include:

- Managers whose operation will be affected.

- Experts who can provide measurement and guidance.

- End users who will have to live with the system. This includes both supporters and resisters.

Finally, ensure that the test results and project progress are communicated broadly and often. Use this as an opportunity to sell your selected solution while it is still undergoing the test phase so as to assure acceptance when it is fully implemented.

CASE EXAMPLE

MANUFACTURING — RAL CHEMICAL CORPORATION

The team's solution, statistical process control, was developed into a goal: to implement statistical process control for the preformers by October 17, 1987, for under $2,000. They didn't believe the solution could be modeled or sample-tested, but instead would require full implementation. They would monitor and measure the success of the solution through weekly quality control reports on the percent of out-of-specification and customer complaints on preforms. They were ready to develop a plan for implementing the solution and meeting their goal.

SERVICE — JAM INSURANCE COMPANY

The solution of redesigning the forms was discussed and stated as a goal: to redesign the policy entry form by January 1, 1988, for under $5,000. The redesigned form would be tested and evaluated for two months by a few people before full implementation. To measure the success of the solution, the errors would be tracked before and after the correction as a percent of entries. The team was ready now to develop a plan for implementing their solution.

7
IMPLEMENTATION

All worthwhile men have good thoughts, good ideas, and good intentions, but precious few of them ever translate them into action.

John Handcock Fields

GENERAL

For many team members, the previous phase of problem solving will have been interesting, challenging, and perhaps even fun. Possible solutions will have been uncovered and narrowed down to a single accepted one, which has been at least minimally tested to show it is a plausible solution.

The difficulty is that implementation is too often slow, dull, and difficult. Creative members of the team who are natural leaders during the earlier stages may well be looking beyond implementation toward the next problem. If forced to stay with the grinding, logical steps of implementation, they may become bored and disinterested. A team composed of individuals of various management styles will find that often the active leadership roles will now be taken over by the more analytically minded types. The key, however, is to ensure that even while logical planning goes forth, you are still being creative, staying interested, and having fun. The ideal solution technique provides an example of such a pathway.

THE IDEAL SOLUTION TECHNIQUE

The problem-solving group can use this creative technique which combines aspects of brainstorming and creative thinking to initialize the group's movement toward a working action plan. While many variations are possible, the ideal solution technique will usually contain the following elements:

1. The group members are asked to create a clear mental image of what they would see, hear, smell, etc., if the solution under question were the ideal one.

2. The images must be converted into physical measurements and accomplishable items.

3. Using the principles and techniques of brainstorming, the individual items are listed, discussed, and evaluated.

4. The group then creates an action plan containing dates, responsibilities, required resources, etc., that will ensure that the ideal solution is achieved. This can be accomplished by moving backward from the ideal position or forward from the actual problem.

CREATING THE ACTION PLAN

The ideal solution technique will have produced not only a visual image of the desired solution, but many individual steps required to move from problem to final solution. The steps need to be converted into an action plan chart which will present the information in a detailed but condensed form.

Many teams are irritated and baffled at this stage by their inability to visualize the whole process while simultaneously documenting each individual's responsibility. For example, two Dallas Cowboy running backs, Herschel Walker and Tony Dorset, were asked the same question: "What did you see when you were handed the football?" Walker replied that he saw only the man immediately in front of him. Dorset, however, said he could see all the remaining 21 players and what each was trying to accomplish. A good action plan should provide the team with the instantaneous Dorset type of vision.

The action plan will ensure that the individual steps selected by the teams are carried to completion in the most effective and efficient manner. It also provides the team, management, and other interested personnel with a detailed, graphic instrument that connotes work activity, time requirements, and the staff responsible for achieving particular results.

While action plans can be as simple as a Gantt Chart, they can be as complex as those provided by the program, evaluation, and review technique (PERT), which was devised to control the complex steps required to complete the Polaris missile program. Regardless of the complexity required for the action plan, it should contain the following essential elements:

1. It must state the activity to be accomplished and break it down into all steps necessary to reach the objective.

2. It must denote a starting and ending point, and determine the total time for completion of the project.

3. It should indicate how the individual activities between starting and finishing points are arranged.

4. It should assign a time for each individual activity.

5. It should assign a person responsible for each activity.

6. It should provide overall coordination via a project manager or equivalent. This person should ensure that the action plan is implemented.

Once the initial plan is established, the team should determine what steps can be eliminated or merged, and what the interaction is between various steps. If it is impossible to eliminate or merge any steps, the group should ask itself whether it can change anything. This opportunity for improvement is one that should not be overlooked when putting together an action plan. Other questions the team should ask include:

- Can we change the sequence?

- Can we change the people responsible?

- Can we improve the action plan in any way to simplify the work and improve the time to complete it?

By making the action plan flexible, the group can ensure its success.

Before finalizing the action plan, the team should involve people outside the team, especially those who could be potential adversaries. Ask for negative responses from the adversarial groups. It will be much easier to handle those negative responses at this time than at a later date. This is an excellent time to get others to interact and to "buy into" the team solution. Once the action plan has been firmed up, it becomes a basic foundation to be used as a sales technique.

SELLING THE ACTION PLAN

Selling is an important, and often overlooked, aspect in problem solving. Because the team believes their solution is the correct one, they often fail to recognize they must still sell this solution and action plan to others.

The first step in selling the team's action plan is to show that the team is enthusiastically committed to the solution. The individual team members should seek opportunities to transfer their enthusiasm to others.

The second step is to understand why others will be willing to accept and support the team solution. Others will buy into the team's solution if the positive is accentuated and the negative eliminated. People will usually ask the question, "What's in it for me?" When they review the team's proposed action plan and solution, they will be looking for those elements that benefit them. This principle was illustrated succinctly in *The One Minute Salesperson* by Johnson[10] in this profound statement: "People don't buy our services, products, or ideas; they buy how they imagine using them will make them feel."

The third step is to get others' attention, often with some type of presentation. It is important for the team to communicate its actions and solutions to various levels within the organization. The better you can speak the language of the various factions involved, the higher the probability of having your solution and action plan accepted.

The checklist presented in Figure 7.1 provides the essential elements that must be discussed and considered so the team's presentation will accomplish its objective. In addition, a nine-step plan for selling an innovative idea is included in Figure 7.2 to serve as a guideline to selling during a presentation.

PRESENTATION CHECKLIST

ANSWER THESE FOUR QUESTIONS:

1. **WHAT DO THE LISTENERS KNOW ALREADY?**

   _____

   _____

2. **WHAT DO THE LISTENERS NEED TO KNOW?**

   _____

   _____

3. **WHY PRESENT THIS MATERIAL AT THIS TIME?**

   _____

   _____

4. **WHAT DOES THE LISTENER NEED TO DO WHEN THE PRESENTATION IS COMPLETED?**

   _____

   _____

Figure 7.1 Presentation checklist.

NINE RULES FOR SELLING
THE INNOVATIVE SOLUTION*

1. **DON'T OVERSELL YOUR SOLUTION**

2. **DON'T GIVE UP TOO SOON**

3. **WATCH YOUR TIMING**

4. **BE BRIEF AND TO THE POINT**

5. **PLAN YOUR PRESENTATION CAREFULLY**

6. **MAKE YOUR SOLUTION ACCEPTABLE**

7. **DRAMATIZE YOUR SOLUTION**

8. **AVOID CONTROVERSY**

9. **PROVIDE FOR DISCUSSION**

Figure 7.2 Nine-step plan for selling an innovative idea. *Adapted from *Applied Problem Solving Through Creative Thinking* by David Reid, American Chemical Society, Washington, DC, 1977.

The fourth step is to ensure that everyone knows the cause and benefits of the team's action plan and solution. The more these benefits can be personalized and directed, the more likely they are to be accepted. Hard data, visual evidence, and references properly presented will help sell the action plan.

IMPLEMENTING THE ACTION PLAN

Now is the time to put the plan into motion — implement it! At times you will want to do a trial implementation to better evaluate whether the full-scale plan will produce the desired results. Other times the final full-scale action plan will be implemented without a trial. Regardless of which option is selected, the following elements should be considered:

1. Identify the affected groups and individuals, brief them, and ask for their cooperation.

2. Prepare cost estimates before and after the solution, if appropriate.

3. Plan for the collection of data.

4. Establish a baseline before the change and use it as a work mark afterwards.

5. Implement the action.

6. Establish and evaluate the baseline after the change.

Orderly, efficient implementation is not an easy task. To assist in this difficult endeavor, Figure 7.3 presents an implementation checklist that the team can use to help prepare for and ensure successful implementation.

Action plans, solutions, and implementation can run into trouble. So it's pertinent to have a refinement plan to deal with new factors, unexpected complications, organizational change, etc. The team must find its own best mixture of planning and improvisation, and then stick to its action plan to gain the best solution.

IMPLEMENTATION CHECKLIST

If action has been completed give evidence of completion. If action has not been completed state further action required (i.e., who, what, when, etc.).

1. Is the proposed solution mapped out from the viewpoint of key people affected by it?

   _____

   _____

2. Have you anticipated any possible sources of resistance to the proposed solution and made plans to overcome that resistance?

   _____

   _____

3. Does management understand changes in work content, procedures, etc. that the solution will create?

   _____

   _____

4. Have you set the critical dates to discuss the implementation progress with key groups?

   _____

   _____

5. Have you listed all the possible positive and negative factors of the proposed program?

   _____

   _____

6. Have you detailed and obtained the resources necessary to achieve total implementation?

   _____

   _____

7. Have you identified milestones (ways of knowing that you are reaching your objective)?

   _____

   _____

8. Have the implementation steps been accomplished on time and does the final product agree favorably with your goal or objective statement?

   _____

   _____

Figure 7.3　Implementation Checklist.

CASE EXAMPLES

MANUFACTURING — RAL CHEMICAL CORPORATION

The team took its time to lay out a plan for implementing its solution. It first discussed what major steps would be needed and then, through consensus, ordered the steps along with assigning responsibilities, time to complete, and start/finish dates. Figure 7.4 shows one of the planning — key steps cards. Figure 7.5 illustrates in a flow diagram the entire key steps' plan. With the plan developed for the team's solution, the only remaining step was to ensure its longevity.

SERVICE — JAM INSURANCE COMPANY

The team had a solution and ways to measure its effectiveness. Now they needed a plan to implement it. It took several meetings to discuss and brainstorm the major steps. Through consensus, the steps were ordered, responsibilities assigned, and times to complete and start/finish dates were established. Figure 7.6 illustrates one of these steps and the cards used to lay out the plan. The major steps in the final action plan are shown in Figure 7.7. The final phase of the DISTIL process was to ensure the longevity of the solution.

PLANNING - KEY STEPS

No. 3

KEY WORDS: DATA & PREPARATION

EXPLANATION: GATHER EXAMPLE DATA &
PREPARE TRAINING MATERIALS

_____ BY R. Clark

Assigned to: C. McBride
Monitored by: J. Smith
Time to Complete: 2 Weeks
Start date: 8-1-87   Finish Date: 8-27-87

Figure 7.4 Planning in key steps card (RAL Chemical Corporation).

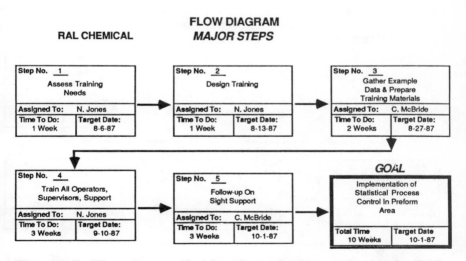

FLOW DIAGRAM
RAL CHEMICAL   **MAJOR STEPS**

Step No. 1		
Assess Training Needs		
Assigned To:	N. Jones	
Time To Do: 1 Week	Target Date: 8-6-87	

Step No. 2		
Design Training		
Assigned To:	N. Jones	
Time To Do: 1 Week	Target Date: 8-13-87	

Step No. 3		
Gather Example Data & Prepare Training Materials		
Assigned To:	C. McBride	
Time To Do: 2 Weeks	Target Date: 8-27-87	

Step No. 4		
Train All Operators, Supervisors, Support		
Assigned To:	N. Jones	
Time To Do: 3 Weeks	Target Date: 9-10-87	

Step No. 5		
Follow-up On Sight Support		
Assigned To:	C. McBride	
Time To Do: 3 Weeks	Target Date: 10-1-87	

GOAL

Implementation of Statistical Process Control In Preform Area	
Total Time 10 Weeks	Target Date 10-1-87

Figure 7.5 Flow diagram showing the entire key step's plan for RAL Chemical Corporation.

```
┌─────────────────────────────────────────────────────────┐
│   ┌─────────────────────────────────────┐               │
│   │     PLANNING - KEY STEPS            │   No.   3     │
│   └─────────────────────────────────────┘               │
│                                                          │
│   KEY WORDS:   TEST RUN                                  │
│                                                          │
│   EXPLANATION:   USING REDESIGNED                        │
│   FORM - PRINT LIMITED AMOUNT                            │
│   AND TEST WITH A FEW SELECTED                           │
│   PEOPLE                          BY    L. Smith         │
│                                                          │
│   Assigned to:  B. Clark                                 │
│   Monitored by:  L. Smith                                │
│   Time to Complete:   8 Weeks                            │
│   Start date:  9-1-87        Finish Date:   11-1-87      │
└─────────────────────────────────────────────────────────┘
```

Figure 7.6 Planning in key steps (JAM Insurance Company).

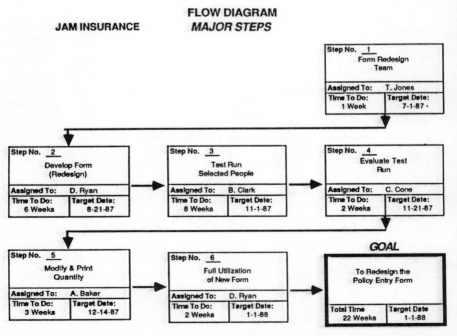

Figure 7.7 Flow diagram showing the key steps for the entire plan (JAM Insurance Company).

8
LONGEVITY

The race is not to the swiftest, but to he who endures to the perfect end.

Isaiah Jones

GENERAL

The team's work is not finished when the solution has been fully implemented. True corrective action deals with correcting the system, not just the immediate problem. The team should develop a plan to track the implemented action to ensure that, when reviewed after a period of time, the expected results are still pertinent and satisfactory. The time to make this plan is during the implementation stage.

The team shoud discuss established criteria, set measurements, and assign individuals to track the solution. One of the most often asked questions is, "What proof is there of success?" Whenever possible, solutions should be tied to cost-of-quality or other improvement measurements that are routinely gathered and distributed. The team's interaction with accounting personnel can aid in establishing cost/benefit reports that depict dollars and time savings, directly and indirectly.

It is often necessary to determine whether the solution has produced any adverse affects. For example, a laboratory-based team used the DISTIL process to solve the problem of used toxic solvents in the laboratory area. Their solution, which was readily accepted by management, was to collect used solvent at the end of each day, place it in proper containers and transport it to appropriate drums in the plant maintenance area. Problem solved! However, when the group reviewed their solution after six months, they determined that they had simply shifted their problem from a small laboratory buildup of used solvents to a large, drum-sized buildup in the maintenance department. Subsequently, by involving maintenance personnel in the team's problem solving and action plans, they found a true solution.

While presentations are often used to gain management approval, there should also be a followup presentation to satisfy management that the suggested solution has, in effect, really worked. Visual evidence provided by films, videos, or photographs are strong evidence of success. Cost/benefit data, properly documented, will also provide strong evidence that the solution will be long lasting. A formal or informal survey on people's perception of the problem and its solution can provide evidence for less tangible types of benefits. A frank testimonial from those closely associated with the problem and its solution can be a powerful tool for showing that the true problem has been solved. The checking process for longevity must be continued until there is virtually no chance that the problem will recur. A longevity checklist (Figure 8.1) will accomplish this.

LONGEVITY CHECKLIST

1. Is there proof that the action is successful?

_____

_____

2. Have adverse effects occurred?

_____

_____

3. Is there a need for additional action?

_____

_____

4. Is management satisfied that the problem has been corrected? _____

_____

_____

5. Are cost/benefit savings expected?

_____

_____

_____

Figure 8.1   Longevity checklist.

When the checklist has been completed and the long-term solution has been properly implemented and the positive effects noted, CONGRATULATIONS! DISTIL has helped you complete your project and...YOUR PROBLEM IS SOLVED!

CASE EXAMPLES

MANUFACTURING — RAL CHEMICAL COMPANY

The last phase of the DISTIL problem-solving process was to discuss and assign followup dates. These dates corresponded with the finish dates for the key steps of the plan, plus later dates after the plan is completed, to ensure it is working and doing as the team expected. The entire DISTIL process was summarized along with the longevity dates, as shown in Figure 8.2. The summary was an excellent, concise reference for discussing the problem-solving process with nonteam members. This completed the DISTIL process for this team's problem...one that was solved by the power of TEAMWORK!

DISTIL SUMMARY

RAL CHEMICAL
(Production)

DEFINE - "THE PROBLEM"

D | High Reject Rates - Out of Weight Specifications Preforms |

IMAGE - THE PROBABLE CAUSES

I

| Poor Training |
| Process Variation |
| Equipment Variation |
| Confusing Instructions |
| |
| |

SELECT - THE MOST LIKELY CAUSE & BEST POSSIBLE SOLUTION

S

| **Cause =** Process Variation |
| **Solution =** Statistical Process Control (SPC) |

TEST - OUR GOAL or OBJECTIVE & TESTS

T

| **Goal =** To Implement SPC for the Preformers by 10-1-87 for under $2000 |
| **Tests =** QC To monitor % weight out of specification, weekly reports |
| QA to report & document customer complaints (preform related) |
| Control Chart Preformers |

IMPLEMENT - THE MAJOR STEPS

I

1. Training Needs, Assess	5. On sight support
2. Design Training	6. Full SPC Implementation
3. Example Data & Training Materials	7.
4. Training	8.

LONGEVITY – THE FOLLOWUP DATES

L

1.	2.	3.	4.	5.	6.	7.	8.
8/27/87	10/1/87	1/4/88	4/1/88	10/1/88			

Figure 8.2 DISTIL summary and longevity dates, for RAL Chemical Corporation.

SERVICE — JAM INSURANCE COMPANY

The data processing team entered the last phase of the DISTIL team process needing only followup dates to monitor progress. They discussed and assigned dates corresponding to the finish dates for the key steps of the plan, plus dates for later followup. The entire DISTIL process was summarized along with the longevity dates, as shown in Figure 8.3. This summary also makes an excellent reference for discussing the team's problem-solving steps with anyone outside the team. Thanks to teamwork and the DISTIL process, the data processing team identified and solved their problem using the power and creativity of the team.

JAM INSURANCE
(Data Processing)

DISTIL — SUMMARY

DEFINE - "THE PROBLEM"

D

TO REDUCE THE POLICY ENTRY ERRORS

IMAGE - THE PROBABLE CAUSES

I

Insufficient Data Entry Clerks
Policy Flow Between Departments
Poorly Designed Forms
Illegible Writing

SELECT - THE MOST LIKELY CAUSE & BEST POSSIBLE SOLUTION

S

Cause =	Poorly Designed Forms
Solution =	To internally redesign forms

TEST - OUR GOAL or OBJECTIVE & TESTS

T

Goal = To redesign the policy entry form by 1-1-88 for under $5000
Tests = Initial sampling to selected people
measured by before + after data on entry errors

IMPLEMENT - THE MAJOR STEPS

I

1. Form Team	5. Modify & Print
2. Develop Form	6. Full Utilization of New Design
3. Test Run	7.
4. Evaluate Test Run	8.

LONGEVITY – THE FOLLOWUP DATES

L

1.	2.	3.	4.	5.	6.	7.	8.
11/1/87	12/14/87	1/14/88	6/1/88	1/1/89			

Figure 8.3 DISTIL summary and longevity dates for JAM Insurance Company.

APPENDIX — CASE STUDY

The example that follows indicates how the TAPS-DISTIL process can convert a nebulous, general, *big mess* problem into a specific problem that a team can tackle productively.

A New Hampshire-based operation of a specialty chemical corporation had experienced rapid growth because of market expansion and acquisitions. With the rapid growth had come a myriad of indicators of customer dissatisfaction, indicated by increased complaints and returns, negative sales force feedback, and letters from major customers. A multilevel, quality improvement team containing individuals from operation management to factory workers was convened and accepted the mission of reducing and controlling this problem.

Definition: The objective of the first step in DISTIL is to reduce one general problem area, such as customer dissatisfaction, to a specific problem or problems that, if corrected, would have a significant impact in reducing the overall negative effect.

To "prime the mental pump," the team begins brainwriting, i.e., individual team members place three or four ideas on sheets of paper. The papers are exchanged and reviewed. The reviewer adds new ideas sparked by the list and the process continues.

The brainwriting ideas are placed on an appropriate chart to serve as the basis for a classic brainstorming session. If any idea was suggested by more than one person, this is indicated on the brainstorming chart and, with consensus of the team, it will receive special consideration during the voting at the end of the brainstorming session.

All rules which normally apply to brainstorming are adhered to and, after adequate discussion, the team votes to identify the top 15 percent of the suggested problems. Figure A.1 shows the top items selected as possible causes for customer dissatisfaction.

To identify the Pareto "vital few," affinity analysis is applied to the top 15 percent of the list. Affinity analysis is a nonverbal method that sorts items according to their affinity between themselves and is used to clarify a chaotic situation. Besides providing a systematic method of ranking the problems, it also allows the team to break away from tradition by removing some of the traditional concepts that block thoughts. It also fosters participation by increasing the team's interaction.

BRAINSTORMING LIST: DISSATISFIED CUSTOMERS

1. Price (Cost) too high
2. Delivery not on time
3. Poor quality products or service
4. Not what was wanted or expected
5. Naturally dissatisfied customer
6. Poor communication
7. Inability to get answers
8. Inadequate design
9. Poor service
10. Packaging not right
11. Appearance unacceptable
12. Performance not acceptable

Figure A.1   Brainstorming list of top 15 percent of items selected as possible causes for customer dissatisfaction.

```
┌─────────────────────────────────────────────────────────────┐
│                   QUALITY TECHNICS                          │
│                         TAPS                                │
│                                                             │
│  IDEA: (Keyword)              QUALITY                       │
│                                                             │
│  Explanation: Material does not meet                        │
│  customer's  expectation                                    │
│                                                             │
│                  By: William  Jones                         │
│                                                             │
│  ┌───────────────────────────────────────────────────────┐ │
│  │              TAPS PRIORITY INDEX                      │ │
│  ├────────┬───────┬───────┬──────────┬─────────┬─────────┤ │
│  │  Type  │ Time  │ Cost  │ Success  │ Quality │  Total  │ │
│  ├────────┼───────┼───────┼──────────┼─────────┼─────────┤ │
│  │   2    │   3   │   1   │    2     │    3    │   10    │ │
│  ├────────┴───────┼───────┴──────────┼─────────┴─────────┤ │
│  │   Individual   │  Assigned To:    │       RMT         │ │
│  │    Problem     ├──────────────────┼───────────────────┤ │
│  │                │  Controlled By:  │       LNJ         │ │
│  └────────────────┴──────────────────┴───────────────────┘ │
└─────────────────────────────────────────────────────────────┘
```

Figure A.2   TAPS affinity analysis card.

The team selects the top (four or five) priority categories, such as type of problem, time to implement, cost to implement, probability of success, impact on quality, etc. The ideas are transferred to TAPS idea cards (Figure A.2) which contain an evaluation chart.

Header cards indicating high, medium or low priority are placed on a table and the team, without discussion, silently separates the cards into one of the given levels. Silent interaction is continued until a team consensus is achieved. The ratings are converted to a numeric scale and placed on the card under the appropriate heading. After all categories have been evaluated, the overall impact of the particular problem is calculated.

Figure A.3 shows the affinity analysis results for the top 15 percent of the customer dissatisfaction area. In this case "delivery not on time" was selected as the prime problem.

EVALUATION CHART

PROBLEMS LIST	TIME	SUCCESS	QUALITY	COST	TYPE			YOUR TOTAL	TEAM TOTAL
	CRITERIA *								
1. DELIVERY NOT ON TIME	1	2	1	1	2				7
2. PRODUCT QUALITY	2	1	1	2	2				8
3. COMMUNICATION	3	1	1	1	3				9
4. PRICE	2	3	2	1	3				11
5. PACKAGE	2	3	2	3	3				13
6. SERVICE	3	3	2	2	3				13
7.									
8.									
9.									
10.									
11.									
12.									
13.									
14.									

*USE: 1-Good, Easy, Short; 2-Average; 3-Poor, Hard, Long

Figure A.3 Affinity analysis for the top 15 percent of the customer dissatisfaction area.

Image: In the image step in the TAPS-DISTIL process, the team, as a group and as individuals, uses its imagination, creativity, and logic to determine the causes and effects of the problem. While this can be achieved using classic cause-and-effect procedures, the DISTIL process uses a slightly different approach, which combines individual and team input with interaction techniques.

The major categories for cause-and-effect (i.e., the four Ms) are selected by the team and a color code is assigned to each. During a five-minute period, the team members individually brainwrite on Post-it Notes™ the possible causes. The note containing the cause is then placed on the appropriate "bone" of the cause-and-effect diagram. Each member observes what has been compiled. Duplicates are simply stacked together.

This brainwriting/cause-and-effect procedure is repeated until the "ideas bank" has been drained. The team then consolidates, rearranges, or modifies the diagram. In this manner, a flexible, meaningful fishbone diagram is created. In some instances, new major or subcategories are developed. The cause-and-effect/image diagram should, at this stage, contain all the probable causes which have come from the logical and creative work of the entire team.

Selection: At this point it is necessary to select the most probable cause from the many possible causes. While the classic voting technique is used, it is not used as the final selector, but only to select the top four or five candidates. Those top candidates are thoroughly researched and discussed.

Figure A.4 depicts the cause-and-effect diagram for the late delivery problem and the consensus voting indicates the top four items as items A-D. Often it is advantageous to appoint subgroups to study and gather data on each of the candidate areas to be presented to the whole team before the final selection process. Delayed ideation is desirable and often a must at this point. For complex problems an article entitled *Computer Aided Cause and Effect Analysis*[11] can be used to analyze factors statistically and create visual aids for presentation of final results.

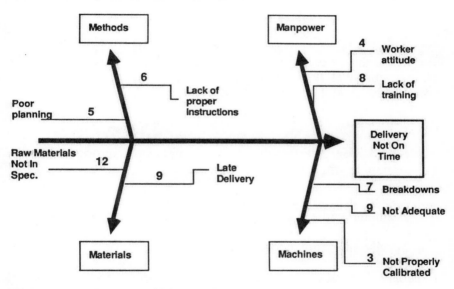

Figure A.4 Cause-and-effect analysis.

The final selection is achieved by creating a priority index (PI). After the reports and discussion phase have been completed, the team members individually rank the top four, and the compiled results are summarized on a form similar to that shown in Figure A.5. In this case, "raw materials not in specification" was selected as the factor to be addressed.

TEAM RANKINGS

PROBABLE CAUSES - KEYWORDS	RANKING								TOTAL
	1.	2.	3.	4.	5.	6.	7.	8.	
A. RAW MATERIAL NOT IN SPECIFICATION	5	2	2	1					19
B. LATE DELIVERY	1	2	4	3					29
C. LACK OF TRAINING	2	6	1	1					21
D. EQUIPMENT NOT ADEQUATE	0	3	4	3					30
E.									
F.									
G.									
H.									

Figure A.5 Team ranking of top four probable causes.

Test: At this point we must test the alternate solutions to select the best one. But first a goal or objective must be established that is acceptable to the entire team. Much has been written about goal setting, but the following simple rules should be complied with:

1. Start with the word "to," followed by an action verb.

2. Specify a single key result to be accomplished that answers a question beginning with "what" or "what kind."

3. Specify a measure of accomplishment that answers a question beginning with "how much," "how long," or "how well."

4. Specify a target date for accomplishment.

Example: To improve the relationship with our top 25 vendors by the end of the third quarter with a cost not to exceed $____.

Various alternate solutions are evaluated by a solution selection matrix (Figure A.6) to determine the best one.

SOLUTION SELECTION CHART

MOST PROBABLE CAUSE - RAW MATERIALS NOT IN SPECIFICATION

POSSIBLE SOLUTIONS	Fixes The Root Cause (Yes/No)	Creates New Problems (Yes/No)	Management Receptivity (Yes/No)	Group Can Implement (Yes/No)	Cost (High/Low)
TIGHTEN-UP INCOMING INSPECTION	NO	YES	YES	YES	HIGH
FIND NEW VENDOR	NO	NO	NO	YES	?
REWORK MATERIAL IN-HOUSE	NO	YES	NO	NO	HIGH
WORK WITH VENDOR TO IMPROVE QUALITY	YES	NO	YES	YES	LOW
FIRE QC MANAGER & INSPECTORS	NO	YES	NO	NO	?

Figure A.6   Solution selection matrix.

The team was selected to work with the vendor to improve the vendor's quality system and product. A vendor day was conducted which allowed for mutual openness and structured discussion of quality needs and expectations. This forum with key vendors produced a better understanding and increased the quality of incoming material.

Implementation: The objective is to get from the most likely solution to the ideal situation, and to create the specific action steps — properly arranged and designated — to allow individuals to complete the desired action.

In the DISTIL process the members are asked to imagine what would be the situation if the selected action were fully implemented and in place, and the problem was corrected. Members picture in their minds what they would see, hear, feel, perceive, etc., and these images are converted into descriptive words during a brainstorming session. While team members may say they work to solve problems, to improve products, service, and profits, they really are motivated by how they imagine they will feel when the problem has been corrected and they are receiving praise or rewards from the team, management, or others.

The picture is set. They know how it should be when the problem is solved. Now the question is, "How do we get there?" An action plan with the major steps must be developed by the team. Starting with the composite ideal imaged situation for the team, the objective is to work backwards in individual action steps to the most likely cause.

A flow diagram will be created which will ensure that the selected action plan is viable and can be effectively carried out to completion. It will also provide a graphic method which indicates the activities, time requirements, and people responsible for achieving the end results.

Once the action plan steps have been completed and the results evaluated, it is important to communicate the team's action and solution to various levels and functions in the organization. They need to know not only what the corrective action will be, but how and why the final conclusions were reached. The presentation should be a team effort. Everyone participated in the problem analysis and solution, and everyone should be involved in some manner in the presentation.

Longevity: The team's work is not over when it implements the corrective action and makes its presentation. It is the team's responsibility to ensure that its action actually does what it was hoped it would do, and that the solution is long lasting and mutually beneficial. The team should develop a plan to track the implementation as a part of the problem-solving process. The team should determine criteria, establish measures, and designate an individual to track the corrective action. Figure A.7 provides a longevity checklist which can aid in tracking the long-lasting effects of the team's solution.

LONGEVITY CHECKLIST

1. Is there proof that the action is successful?

Higher % of Incoming Material in Specification

2. Have adverse effect occurred?
NO

3. Is there a need for additional action?
NO

4. Is management satisfied that the problem has been corrected?
Yes, Management Has Received Postive
Customer Feedback.

5. Are cost/benefit savings expected?
Yes, Quarterly Accounting Report Indicates Cost
Saving 110% of Projection

Figure A.7   Longevity checklist for monitoring project.

REFERENCES

1. Toffler, Alvin. *Future Shock*. New York: Random House, 1970.

2. Naisbitt, John. *Megatrends*. New York: Warner Books, Inc., 1982.

3. Kanter, Rosabeth Moss. *The Change Masters: Innovation and Entrepreneurship in the American Corporation*. New York: Simon & Shuster, 1983.

4. Ouchi, William G. *Theory Z*. Reading, Mass.: Addison-Wesley Publishing Co., 1981.

5. Peters, Tom, and Robert H. Waterman. *In Search of Excellence*. New York: Warner Books, 1983.

6. Kern, Jill P., John J. Riley, and Louis N. Jones. *Human Resource Management*. New York: Marcel Dekker, 1987.

7. Jongeward, D., and P. Seyer. *Choosing Success*. New York: John Wiley & Sons, Inc., 1987.

8. Gordon, Thomas. *Leader Effectiveness Training*. New York: G.P. Putnam's Sons, 1977.

9. Osborne, A.F. *Applied Imagination — The Principles and Problems of Creative Problem Solving*. New York: Charles Scribner's Sons, 1953.

10. Johnson, S., and L. Wilson. *The One-Minute Salesperson*. New York: William Morrow and Co., Inc., 1985.

11. Jones, Louis N. "Computer Aided Cause and Effect Analysis." *40th Annual Conference Transactions*. Northeastern Quality Control Conference, 1986.

BIBLIOGRAPHY

Biondi, A.M. *The Creative Process*. Buffalo, N.Y.: DOK Publishers, 1972.

Dixon, Wilfred J., and Frank J. Massey, Jr. *Introduction to Statistical Analysis*. New York: McGraw-Hill Book Co., 1982.

Francis, D., and D. Young. *Improving Work Groups*. San Diego: University Associates, 1979.

Grant, Eugene L., and Richard S. Leavenworth. *Statistical Quality Control*. McGraw-Hill Book Co., 1972.

Hayes, Glenn E., and Harry G. Romig. *Modern Quality Control*. Encino, Calif.: BRUCE, 1977.

Ishikawa, Kaoru. *Guide to Quality Control*, 2nd ed. Tokyo: Asian Productivity Organization, 1982.

Jones, Louis N., and Ronald C. McBride. "Team Approach to Problem Solving." *41st Annual Quality Congress Transactions*, American Society for Quality Control, 1987.

McBride, Ronald C. "Vendor Day — A Human Resource Technique." *42nd Annual Quality Congress Transactions*, American Society for Quality Control, 1988.

McBride, Ronald C. "The Selling of Quality." *41st Annual Quality Congress Transactions*, American Society for Quality Control, 1987.

Parnos, S.J., R.B. Noller, and A.M. Biondi. *Guidebook to Creative Action*. New York: Charles Scribner's Sons, 1976.

Pfeiffer, J.W., and J.E. Jones. *The Handbook of Structured Experience*. San Diego: University Associates, 1977.

Reid, David. *Applied Problem Solving Through Creative Thinking*. Washington, D.C.: American Chemical Society, 1977.

INDEX